# GHOSTS OF MARTHA'S VINEYARD

# GHOSTS OF MARTHA'S VINEYARD

## THOMAS DRESSER

### FOREWORD BY HOLLY NADLER

Haunted America

Published by Haunted America
A Division of The History Press
Charleston, SC
www.historypress.com

First published 2020

Manufactured in the United States

ISBN 9781467146463

Library of Congress Control Number: 2020938583

Ghosts of Martha's Vineyard *is dedicated to the late John Alley,*
*historian, raconteur and Vineyard character.*

# CONTENTS

# FOREWORD

**W**ay before I wrote my first ghost books, my fascination with the paranormal started in London, and specifically, it started with walking tours.

Hard as it is to believe today, what with ghost stories having flourished all over America like an invasion of something piquant but distinctly foreign, back in 1983, when I paid a visit to my folks who lived in my uncle Marshall's apartment in Cadogan Square in London, I'd never heard of walking tours devoted to haunted locales. Or anything else, really.

Now bear in mind that the English, who've been happily walking since well before the Battle of Hastings, had for a long time been offering rambles through town on all subjects. Georgian architecture, anyone? Pub crawls of the Bloomsbury Circle? At least two dozen walks were on offer, mostly for the delectation of tourists, mostly about history and the arts, and they were dutifully listed in the paper.

I loved the very idea of these footloose lectures, so when my parents suggested we take a couple, I accepted the list presented in the paper and circled the ones that drew me in above all others.

1. *Follow in the Footsteps of Jack the Ripper*
2. *The Ghosts of London*

Let's just say I've got a passion for exciting stories. Jack the Ripper attacks took place at night, and we indeed followed in his tracks where the bodies were long ago discovered. His primary hood, Whitechapel, was as dark and grimy and dispiriting in 1983 as it had been in the 1890s, and at one point, my mom said loudly, as she was wont to do whenever an occasion to embarrass anyone in her family developed, "What are we doing in Whitechapel?"

But even more entertaining was an afternoon ramble devoted to haunted London. As we know, England itself has always been home to more ghostly haunts than fish 'n' chips joints. The story that stayed with me involved the gorgeous acres of Green Park. Some centuries ago during one of the major plague years, this spot, now in the heart of town, lurked out in the country where a tremendous pit was dug for wagons hauling new corpses for discard. These days, such a long time later, a sense of melancholy still hovers over the greensward. No picnickers are able to linger, and no flowers grow.

Many years later, in the early '90s, my beloved (now) ex-husband Marty, with our seven-year-old son, Charlie, moved to the Vineyard year-round, having lived and worked in LA in the TV comedy biz. One of the gigs I took on for myself was to provide walking tours for the visitors of summer.

I intuited that Edgartown would be rife with ghost stories, so the *Ghosts of Edgartown* went on the docket. I also developed *From Camp Meet to Cat House: The Sacred and Profane Oak Bluffs* and *The Rich and Famous of Vineyard Haven*. When the first tour pulled in five times as many walkers, I realized the other two down-island towns had their share of ghoulies as well, and all three town tours featured *Ghosts* in their titles.

What I discovered, and assuredly my friend and colleague Tom Dresser has as well, is that when you put out the call for true local ghost stories, islanders practically take a number to tell you theirs. I've even found explanations why old New England towns are so very spookified. Researchers of the paranormal will tell you that ghosts are enhanced and telecommunicated by electric energy and thereby along water channels. Our towns on the waterfront, with their fogs and shallow aquifers, dial up those occult figures like no other geographical settings.

Plus, just as the UK has specialized in haunted sites from so many centuries of history and the sheer volume of stories that vie for attention, we're starting to collect, in older parts of our country, our own versions of Anne Boleyn with 'er 'ead tucked underneath her arm—although, so far nothing quite that lurid.

What I told Tom when he was starting out with these ghost tales for The History Press is that he'd find almost all the reports believable. It's about community and being accountable to one another. Naturally, we have our crazies and our exaggerators, but for the most part, the friends and neighbors who regale you with the time a ghost made green pancakes to celebrate St. Paddy's Day, you know it happened. It really happened.

So enjoy the following true stories. I myself stand eager to see what new eerie spirits are visiting these shores.

—Holly Nadler, author of *Haunted Island*, *The Ghosts of Boston Town*, *Vineyard Confidential* and *Vineyard Supernatural*

# ACKNOWLEDGEMENTS

T om, full blessings to pursue your own ghost book!" said Holly Nadler, the Ghost Lady of Martha's Vineyard.

Historian/teacher Chris Baer said, "Sounds like fun, Tom! I'm no believer in the supernatural, but I may have a few tales for you."

"What a fantastic topic. I will look through our files and see what I can come up with for you!" commented Hilary Wallcox, librarian of the *Vineyard Gazette*.

Liz Villard, the maven of Edgartown history, said, "You realize that your tape recorder jammed after we discussed the fact that Jasper's recorder jammed. Hmmm."

Martha's Vineyard Museum librarian Bow Van Riper wrote, "I've heard a lot of St. Pierre Camp alums say that the Marine Hospital felt spooky."

"A ghost led an incomplete life," said paranormal Karen Coffey. "A ghost leaves a piece of itself in the old house. It is like a black-and-white negative."

"Some people enjoy their best accomplishments in retirement," said Victoria Haeselbarth. "They bloom into their full glory."

And Jim Chirgwin, who grew up in the Daggett House, perhaps the most haunted house on Martha's Vineyard, added this caveat: "Have fun!"

WITH THE SUPPORT AND encouragement of a vast array of Vineyarders, how could I not pursue this unique topic? My thanks to John Alley, Chris Baer, Catie Blake, Joan Boykin, Nan Byrne, Jim Chirgwin, Amy Coffey, Karen Coffey, Gary Cook, Susan Desmarais, Patty Egan, Cynthia Farrington, Frank

Fenner, Victoria Haeselbarth, Donna Humphrey, Robyn Joubert, Holly Nadler, David, Elena and Steven Perzanowski, Jim Powell, Greer Thornton, Liz Villard, Hilary Wallcox, Tara Whiting-Wells, Susan Wilson and Robyn Wingate.

To The History Press crowd, I so enjoy working with commissioning editor Mike Kinsella, copyeditor Abigail Fleming and marketeer maven Dani McGrath as well as myriad supporting actors and agents along the way.

In addition to the above listed people, I express my sincere appreciation to my wife, Joyce, who was with me every step of the way, from the first bar scene experience at the Kelley House to the last luncheon with a ghost hunter in South Carolina. Joyce took the majority of photographs. Joyce edited the manuscript. Joyce supported me on this haunting journey. I leaned on her spiritual shoulder throughout the process; now it's up to the reader to savor the rewards.

# Prologue

artha's Vineyard's history, along with its fair share of strange occurrences, makes it a major hub for ghost hunters and local storytellers alike. Whether you're fully in touch with the spirit world or you're a little skeptical, the Vineyard is rife with amazing coincidences, strange experiences and unknown mysteries.[1]

That so many guests, employees, locals and visitors have experienced a visit from beyond gives credence to the basic premise that we don't really know or understand everything that's happening around us.

We begin our adventures of haunted happenings with a visit to Edgartown, the first island settlement by Europeans, in 1642. The majority of the haunted sites we investigate are historic inns or hotels, perfect locales for a spectral spirit to stake out a claim for eternity ."Martha's Vineyard is known for its rich history, with many buildings and houses dating back to the early 1600s. Because of this, tales have been told, and visitors have shared 'sightings' of mysterious things. If you're a fan of ghost stories, it's lots of fun to hear them and decide for yourself if it's true!"[2]

We offer firsthand experiences; some doubtful events and a few unexplained circumstances on our journey. Bear with us—some, indeed many, of the sightings that follow cannot be explained away by conventional means. The people who related these tales are serious, sincere and consistent in what they saw, heard and felt. We have no reason to doubt their stories.

A couple of caveats are in order. Some people are sensitive about sharing paranormal experiences. If you want to visit one of sites mentioned in this book, we ask that you respect the owner's privacy. Not everyone is open to ghost stories; not everyone wants to be accused of making up tales.

A second note is that we uncovered ghost stories in several buildings across the island not mentioned here. Not everyone wants to share an unseen dog rubbing against a hotel guest's leg or a sudden draft rustling a customer's hair. Several entrepreneurs requested anonymity or exclusion from this publication. That does not mean they do not have spectral stories; it means they don't want them publicized. We respect their privacy.

Our most vivid advice in sharing these tales is to not be afraid and to have fun with these tales.

# 1
# EDGARTOWN

Charles Banks, the preeminent Vineyard historian who researched and wrote a definitive three-volume early history of the Vineyard in 1911, defined the import of colonial inns: "Under the colonial laws of Massachusetts each town was obliged to keep a 'house of entertainment' for the convenience of strangers, and in 1656 each town was made liable for not keeping an 'ordinary,' as taverns were called in those days."[3]

In each village, the innkeeper was charged with providing entertainment to those travelers who stayed at his inn. An innkeeper held a license to serve beer or wine yet needed a second license to serve hard alcohol. And innkeepers were prohibited from selling alcohol to Indians.

Jim Chirgwin's family has been a presence in the Edgartown hotel business for more than a century. His paternal grandfather, Edgartown native Thomas Henry Chirgwin, embarked on a new career in the early years of the twentieth century when he switched from plumber to innkeeper. In 1911, he opened the Colonial Inn (now Vineyard Square) on North Water Street. Jim's parents assumed management of the Daggett House, also on North Water Street, and ran it for decades. Jim grew up in the Daggett House, located on the lane where automobiles queue up for the Chappy Ferry.

*The Guide to Martha's Vineyard*, published by the *Vineyard Gazette*, described the Daggett House, specifically the lower level:

> *The room was the first tavern on Martha's Vineyard to sell beer and ale. In 1660 the taverner, John Daggett, was fined five shillings for "selling strong*

*liquor." In 1750 the Daggett House was added to the building. Through the years the Daggett House was a custom's house, a sailor's boardinghouse, a store, and during the whaling era, a counting house.*

A few more words from Charles Banks: "The sentimental memories which cluster around these historic inns is rather one of good cheer, warm hospitality, and a mug of hot flip as a fitting close to the day's sojourn."[4] Appreciate these words when you drop in for a hot flip at the Newes from America, the pub at the Kelley House.

Banks, again, from his 1911 tome: "We will close the scene with his last encomium, the epitaph, as it was written of John Doggett, a native of the Vineyard, who dispensed tavern hospitality in his later days." Not sure if this refers specifically to the Daggett House, but it could. A bit of doggerel completes the tale:

*Who when alive so well did Tend,*
*The Rich, the Poor, the Foe, the Friend*
*How oft doth man by care oppressed,*
*Find in an inn a place of rest.*

For decades, the Daggett House was known for its popular Grape-Nuts toast. Joan B. recalled, "I stayed a few times at the Daggett House Inn before it was renovated and turned into a private residence. One of the things I remember most is their famous Grape Nut bread/toast." She added, "I stayed at the Daggett House twice…once in the main house and once in the charming two-room house in the garden. It was one of the nicest bed-and-breakfasts and now is one of the nicest looking homes in Edgartown."

Given the prominence of social media, Karen Kuhfeldt posted about her connection to the Daggett House: "That is my ninth great-grandfather's place. John Daggett came to the colonies in 1630." And Judith Fenton also posted: "My great-great-grandmother was Almira Daggett and a direct descendant of Joseph Daggett. Interesting that there may be a ghost or two in that now residence. I wonder if they bother the owners."

The question whether ghosts once inhabited the Daggett House has arisen over the years. Jim Chirgwin sought to put such stories to rest: "I really have *no ghost sightings* to report. I grew up in the Daggett House and never heard moan, groan, rustling chains or similar suggestions of the presence of otherworldly spirits."

The fireplace was adjacent to the concealed latch to the secret staircase, leading to a secret room. Can you see the ghosts of the little boys and their dog in the fireplace smoke? *Public domain.*

That said, Jim did raise suspicions of spectral sightings: "George Thibault, our waiter and friend, claimed to have been visited frequently by a Revolutionary War soldier, Hiram, and George was interviewed for several ghost story articles." Unfortunately, Thibault passed away in 2012 and cannot be queried for specific details. However, his experiences are described in detail in Holly Nadler's *Haunted Island*.

Jim Chirgwin added: "One of our managers is probably responsible for starting the ghost stories to entice believers to come to stay at the Daggett House." So just the possibility of a spectral sighting could be enough to boost business, at least from the perspective of the innkeeper.

Another ghostly admission slipped from the lips of Mr. Chirgwin: "One event that stirred imaginations was the time that a young couple checked into our 'secret staircase' room late one night and were never seen again!"

And then we have the words of Karen Coffey, who also spent a night at the Daggett House. On her honeymoon, Karen and her new husband stayed in the bedroom up the secret staircase. She saw someone walking around the bed, and it was not her husband.

A secret staircase? Now we're getting somewhere. When the Daggett House operated as an inn, a secret set of stairs in the lower level ran up beside the fireplace. The stairs led up to a garret room, private, removed and secretive. It would have made a great place to hide from the law, from a friend or family member. So the very possibility of a secret chamber elicits a story or two.

One patron described the scene: "An interesting feature of the Daggett House was its secret room. I'm not sure what it was used for in the 1600s or so but during the past years as a B&B it was a guest room, provided they could find the secret door and providing the *ghost* wasn't in residence!!!"

One had to know where the latch was to open the door to ascend the stairs. The handle was secreted in one of the shelves above cabinets in the bookcase. If you didn't know where the handle was, it was basically invisible; thus no one would know there was access to a room upstairs.

Liz Villard knows the history of Edgartown. She posited that the room could have been used to hide escaped slaves as a station on the Underground Railroad during the nineteenth century. Whaling ships came into Edgartown Harbor, often with sailors whose origins were unknown. A secret room would be ideal for hiding escaped slaves.

In its day, the Daggett House was a premier hostelry and a premier site for ghost hunters. *Photo by Joyce Dresser.*

So what about the ghost?

"One of our guests," said Jim Chirgwin, "took a 'ghost photo,' which, according to the believers, showed a face or faces in the fire in the old fireplace."

Spectral sightings are intriguing.

The mythical saga of two brothers is sad and short. Two young boys lived in the Daggett House eons ago. One boy was sent off to Chilmark to live with the grandparents. Before he left, the first boy hid their dog in the secret staircase, to play a joke on the remaining brother. The second boy did not find the dog, was devastated to lose the dog, took ill and died.

The first boy returned from Chilmark and learned of his brother's death. He opened the door to the secret staircase to find the dog had died of starvation. In anguish, he jumped to his death in the harbor. It is said that people who are aware of the ghosts on Martha's Vineyard can sense the presence of these two young boys and their dog while walking by the Daggett House, which is now a private residence.

A FORMER EMPLOYEE OF the Daggett House, Heidi Raihoffer, has a friend who doesn't believe in ghosts but is never the last to leave the building, just in case. She added that another friend said, "I don't believe in ghosts, but let me tell you what happened," and launched into a tale that is hard to believe.

In the early 2000s, the Daggett House closed down and the building was remodeled into a private home. We're not sure whether any ghosts remain on the premises, but apparently one slipped into the boathouse when it was moved across town.

THIS NEXT STORY IS a literal takeaway from the Daggett House.

When the inn ended operations in the early 2000s, the boathouse down by the harbor was moved several blocks away, to Pierce Lane. The boathouse is relatively small and was attached to the main house. And there it sits.

In the winter of 2017, a local woman rented the property. Her tale includes reports of spectral sounds and movements, although there were no specific sightings.

The boathouse of the Daggett House was moved to Pierce Lane. Apparently, a poltergeist or two moved along too. *Photo by Joyce Dresser.*

Nan Byrne said, "I thought I would pass along a ghostly tidbit." She explained that while she worked in Vineyard Haven, she rented this small house in Edgartown one winter.

Nan wrote, "The house is unusual in that the boat house from the Daggett House (Edgartown Harbor) was moved there. It is pretty much a wooden kitchen, bedroom, and eating area attached now to a modern structure—almost original."

Her description of the interior of the Daggett boathouse continued:

> *From the outside the house looks like one structure but inside when you turn left after entering the house you are in an old wood paneled room with an old fireplace and curved ceiling, a kitchen area, one bedroom with a low*

*loft sleeping area above. The rafters are exposed. There is a rickety stair to the sleeping loft, several cubbies inside the fireplace, a back door, and the infamous (in that it kept unlatching itself) latched closet. If you turn right you are in a modern carpeted living room and upstairs is a huge modern bedroom. There is a door between the two areas. I actually would lock that door when I was there alone!*

The boathouse was listed as a summer rental and carried the following description:

*Originally the boathouse for the Daggett House Edgartown Harbor, this historic cottage was completely renovated in 2002 and in 2004 an addition was built. The original cottage has a gourmet kitchen with Italian tile, a period dining room with curved ceiling overlooking a large stone patio abutting Sheriffs Meadow.*

That is pretty straightforward; nothing out of the ordinary. Nan continued,

*We had lots of what I can only call ghostly doings—noises, footsteps, and lots of unlatching of the closets in that part of the house. Sometimes we would be in the kitchen and hear footsteps in the sleeping loft overhead, or hear the opening closing of doors. Once I had items I set out on the floor re-arranged in a weird pattern.*

There was no logical explanation for these strange sounds and movements except that the Daggett House was the primary site before this boathouse was moved. Perhaps spirits are still connected to the original structure.

Nan recorded the various disturbances, but that information does not seem to be available:

*I used to have a bunch of photos of the house but curiously the morning that we got up to leave the house for good my expensive Mac died and never worked again. It was a logic board failure. :) My photos could not be retrieved.*

~

NEXT WE AMBLE DOWN and across Daggett Lane where the automobiles queue up for the Chappy Ferry. We reach The Anchors, an early twentieth-century structure with a history. Edgartown Council on Aging is housed at The Anchors, which shares a parking lot with the Kelley House and the Ol' Sculpin Gallery.

Our first commentator is Leslie Clapp, director of the Martha's Vineyard Center for Living. We asked her about any spectral sightings at The Anchors. She noted, "My office was on the third floor at the Anchors for over ten years. I've heard the stories—I am a believer in ghosts or spirits in general but never experienced anything there except a general feeling of not wanting to be in my office or in the building alone after dark."

The Anchors sits on the edge of Edgartown Harbor. It is a site for elders to congregate. And for ghostly presences to reside. *Photo by Thomas Dresser.*

Our second correspondent was Susan Desmarais, who also worked at The Anchors. Her office was on the second floor, by the stairs that lead up to the third floor.

Often Susan held meetings after 4:00 p.m. After her clients had left the building, she was the only one still there. She would lock the doors and proceed upstairs to complete her paperwork in the evening quiet.

More than once she was aware of a presence, a spirit that was in the building. She never saw anything, but she is very clear that she felt a presence. And there was no one else in the building.

Susan met a man who used to live at The Anchors, when it was a private home. When she asked him about the spirits, he smiled. He confirmed that there are spirits in the building. They won't hurt you, but they are definitely there.

One evening, Susan held a caregivers meeting in her office. By then, she was well aware of the presence of spirits but didn't share her experience. One person in the group spoke up: "There is a spirit here. I can feel it. Do you know about it?" Susan smiled. "Yes, I know about the spirits, but they won't hurt you."

In the busy activity of the day, the spirits are not active; it's in the quiet at day's end when one can sense their presence.

MY BUDDY HERB, AGE ninety-two, invited me to share the weekly meal with seniors at the Edgartown Council on Aging. He enjoys the socialization of a friendly atmosphere. The environment is conducive to lively chatter, weekly updates and the chance for a decent meal.

I joined Herb for the fellowship but had another item on my agenda. Rumor has it there is a presence on the third floor. I met the council's outreach worker, Victoria Haeselbarth, to investigate these stories.

Victoria led me up two flights of creaky stairs, steps that run up and over the rooms where the healthy meal had just been served. Three tiny offices and a bathroom make up the vacant third floor of The Anchors. Victoria softly explained that people have felt a presence, an unknown energy that may be something more than a rarely used storage area.

Victoria spoke about a spectral presence she had seen. It was "a young male, someone troubled, who sits in the yellow room, making ship models." He could have been sickly and passed away. He could have had a hard time

*Above*: The bathroom on the third floor is cramped, with the tub suitable only for a child. *Photo by Thomas Dresser.*

*Left*: The yellow room is where the lost and lonely ghost of a young man struggles with ship models. *Photo by Thomas Dresser.*

Footsteps have been heard in the hallway at the top of the stairs. Yet no one is up there. *Photo by Thomas Dresser.*

in life and didn't finish what he wanted to do, so he is still here. She admitted to feeling his presence at times when she is up there.

Victoria Haeselbarth was interviewed by Holly Nadler some years ago. At that time, she said,

> *"There's something off about him. He's moving slowly and appears to be struggling with a chore that eludes his mental capacity." She said that when she sees him, she tries to figure out, as a clinician herself, precisely what his condition might be—mental or physical or both.*[5]

The three rooms and tiny bathroom open onto the hallway/landing at the top of the stairs. As I peeked into the bathroom, Victoria explained that a psychic had reported seeing the image of a young girl in the bathtub. (The tub is unusual in that it is tiny—big enough only for a child.)

Victoria's office is on the second floor, adjacent to the bottom step of the second flight of stairs. She has heard sounds. On a windy night, she'll be startled, until she realizes it's the wind blowing against the vents of the building. Yet on very quiet nights, she can be startled by unusual sounds and the strong sense that someone else is in the building. Yet there is no one there.

Late in the afternoon, in the remains of the workday, Victoria is the last to leave. In late autumn, as the sun starts to set, it's dark by the time she closes up. She said she has heard unexplained noises. Sometimes these sounds filter down from upstairs, a bump or a step that cannot be explained. When she leaves her office, only rarely will she glance up the staircase. Her sense that there is another presence in the building occurs every so often, not on a regular basis.

Is it fear of someone or something on the third floor? Victoria doesn't want to be frightened, doesn't want that tap on the shoulder only to find no one is there.

At the end of our talk, Victoria smiled. She said the spectral sightings are fun. As an employee with more than twenty years' service to the senior community of Edgartown, while working at The Anchors, she enjoys her job. Victoria projects a friendly, trusting nature, although she admitted to a lot of scuttlebutt about the unknown presence people feel in the building. She does not want to experience the element of surprise, so she keeps a close eye on all that is around her whenever she has to go up those stairs to those abandoned rooms on the third floor.

She has no doubt there is an unexplained force or energy in the building.

~

We spoke by phone a couple of weeks after my initial visit. Of herself, Victoria said, "I enjoy my work; I find it very gratifying when I can work with a client and bring their health and emotional issues into a safe and secure environment."

On further consideration, Victoria suggested,

> *He seemed to have some sort of disability such as autism, that created great focus for the craft he was undertaking, but there was a sense of his pining or yearning for something; perhaps a voyage at sea, or a sense of belonging in the community. But his thoughts and personality set him up for a more cloistered existence. Someone who had a psychic gift visited The Anchors and she and I concurred.*

Victoria said that the Norton family used to live in the house. Maybe the spectral spirit is a sibling who once lived there. Or, posited Victoria, "perhaps, one of the workers in the icehouse or Manual Swartz's boat building shop came to an untimely end and has left an energy footprint."

When I asked Victoria to tell me exactly what she had seen, she said, "I can only describe what I've seen as indefinable."

To confirm her sightings, her sense of a presence on the third floor, Victoria shared that a person with psychic experience "verified my vision; she says I sensed the energy, the disquietude." This professional described what had caused the sense of a presence in the attic room: the sightings reveal energy, like fingerprints when they are examined by a professional—they leave a ghostly imprint of the past.

Victoria added, "A professional assessed what I had seen. She added components prior to me sharing what I had experienced. It was a psychic experience and very solidifying for me."

Haeselbarth has studied physics, and her beliefs are based on physical evidence. Imprints remain, like fingerprints. Does this energy exist? Energy transforms; it doesn't die. It's like a stain or an imprint; the energy is left behind. People with a disturbed mind can leave that kind of energy behind. Some imprint of that man's psyche was left in the building. The energy or an energetic imprint was left behind. Being receptive allows one to open the door to who they once were. This is the most logical, perceptive and scientific explanation of ghosts I have encountered.

Victoria concluded,

*I used to study meditation, which opened up new channels for me: my writing and art got better. I was more receptive to the energy of plants and animals all around. I've seen the ghost three or four times, sensed the energy. It gives me an unsettled feeling, making me anxious to leave the building. Haven't sensed anything recently, but I've been tied up at work.*

# 2
# I READ THE NEWS TODAY, OH BOY

J ust a short walk from the Daggett House sits the Kelley House, one of the more popular hostelries in Edgartown. Yet it has a reputation for unusual events experienced by both staff and guests. And these events have occurred in guest rooms and in the Newes from America, the iconic pub on the ground floor, founded in 1742.

I'd heard the rumors and read about the Kelley House, so I decided to drop in to the Newes to find out a little more. I sat at the bar with Jeff, a bartender working the evening shift shortly before Thanksgiving. My wife, Joyce, and I had dined at the Newes the night before and been told Jeff had some experience with the supernatural at the Kelley House.

Jeff has worked as a bartender at the Kelley House for two years. He shared a few incidents he could not explain, then referred me to a manager who had other experiences and knowledge of what goes on at the Kelley House. (There was one event he refused to share or discuss in any way. By speaking confidentially to another source, I learned Jeff used to stay in certain room in the old part of the hotel. Short-haired and blond, Jeff was spooked when he found long, dark strands of hair on his bed. And one time he left his door open, wide open. A few moments later, the door slammed shut, without explanation.)

Jeff confirmed a story I had heard from an independent source: Carrie, a former employee, shared, "One night wine glasses came flying off the bar and onto the floor. There were guests there. It's definitely worth investigating." Two wine glasses jumped off the shelf, fell to the floor and broke when no one was near them. Jeff was there when it happened. The glasses were propelled from the shelf behind the bar. They flew more than eight feet out over the bar, fell and smashed on the floor. It was highly unusual and totally unexpected. There was no logical explanation.

Another incident that Jeff shared regarded an incident when an ornament on a Christmas wreath, hanging on the wall, fell off. The ball dropped to the floor of the bar and rolled around. It bounced. Then it rolled in the opposite direction. There was no explanation.

More than once, the fire in the fireplace has been built up in the course of the evening. It adds charm and warmth to the atmosphere. As the evening wanes, the bartender lets the fire die down. On more than one occasion, near closing time, the fire burst out more forcefully, as if it were rekindled, although no one added fuel to the flame. It's as if someone didn't want the evening to end. This experience has amazed the bartender and waitresses, as well as any lingering guests.

The fireplace of the Newes has been known to burn down at the end of the evening. It will suddenly flare up, without warning or assistance. Is Helen trying to tell us something? *Photo by Joyce Dresser.*

The Kelley House sits inauspiciously on North Water Street, with nary a hint of the ghosts within. *Photo by Joyce Dresser.*

The bar at the Newes can be a lively. convivial setting. It is also known to be haunted. *Photo by Joyce Dresser.*

In an offhand way, Jeff mentioned that on occasion a light or two has gone off for no apparent reason. If the bartender waits a few minutes, the light goes back on. The bulbs are tight and good, the wiring in place, the switches untouched. Again, there is no logical explanation for flickering lights, which happen often. Some employees find it disconcerting. This lighting game appears to be neither dangerous nor a malfunctioning electronic device.

Jeff has worked at the bar of the Kelley House since 2017. He witnessed several of these unusual events but is neither frightened nor distraught by the experience. He presents as a serious, stable young man who accepts life as it is. While he cannot explain these events, he is not put off, scared or upset by them.

On another visit to the Newes from America, I sat with Adrianne, a waitress on duty on a cool clear morning in early December. The holidays were a couple of weeks away, but the bar of the Newes from America was full of festive décor.

Adrianne has also worked at the Kelley House for a couple of years. She told me about the lights in the bar going on and off without reason and glasses falling off the shelf in the bar by themselves. She was explicit in describing the Christmas ornament that fell off a wreath, rolled across the room, then whipped back in the opposite direction. "It flew across the room like it was shot."

Even more dramatic was Adrianne's description of the spectral apparition of Helen, the ghost of the wife of a sea captain. Her bedroom was where the captain slept, decades or even a century ago. That would be room 307. "She's very active during the holidays," said Adrianne. Room 307 was on the second floor, when this was a boardinghouse, she explained. Helen was waiting for her husband to come home from his voyage, but he never returned.

Adrianne explained that Helen has been seen standing by the fireplace in the pub. She likes to play with the lights.

*Sometimes when she does something, the hair on the back of my neck stands up, but I'm not afraid of her. One time I was alone here, and heard footsteps and chairs moving in the pub. No one was here, but I heard the sounds. I'm used to it now. She's not angry. She just lets you know she's here. It's really pretty neat.*

When things happen, nothing is broken except glassware. Helen does not seem to be malicious or destructive. Other than a couple of glasses leaping from the shelf and smashing on the floor, and the flickering lights, there's nothing to complain about.

"She plays with the lights a lot. Christmas and Thanksgiving, during the holidays, she's especially active, but not so much in the summer. I've never seen anything like this. She's just letting us know she's here. She's not angry. Around the holidays she's very active."

Confidentially I was told that an employee once stayed in her room and saw her. He was freaked out when the bedroom door opened and closed.

~

ROBYN JOUBERT HAS WORKED at the Kelley House for a number of years and is familiar with both the barroom atmosphere and the hotel.

Robyn Joubert is the general manager of the Newes. She oversees all that is going on and is eager to share what she knows. "Helen is a presence. We know she's around, but we are not afraid."

Robyn has been a member of the Kelley House staff since 1983. How did she end up on the Vineyard? Like so many people, it was for a man.

At nighttime, Robyn heard a ball bouncing on the other side of the wall of the pub. She could anticipate when the ball would bounce against the wall behind her. She had a clear sense that a small boy was playing ball. "It's like I could feel the ball bouncing." Robyn continued: "I caught sight of him out of the corner of my eye." She didn't get a good look at the boy, but the image of what she saw stayed with her.

> *Spirits are preparing the living for the hereafter. I'm from New Orleans. Spirits are a big part of life. I feel very at home here. I never feel uncomfortable. Over the past ten years I've felt Helen's presence. One time I saw her by the fireplace. Her dress was a bluish glow. Once we put brass candlesticks over the fireplace. I knew Helen would not approve. I said, "She's not going to like that." Just like that all the candlesticks fell off the mantel and onto the floor.*

Helen seems to seek Robyn out. "I can feel her. I sit down with a cup of coffee, and I think she likes the companionship." Robyn senses that Helen enjoys the time she shares with her: "You feel her presence, like when someone is staring at you. She really misses people; she's not malicious at all. I believe in spirits and feel very comfortable around her."

Once again, Joyce and I went to dinner at the Newes from America, aka the Kelley House. The room was filled with a boisterous crowd. The hostess, Esther, found us seats at the bar, where we ordered drinks and dinner.

I had shared my spectral sightings stories with my wife. During dinner, Robyn stopped by. I asked her for corroboration on seeing the woman in the bluish dress by the fireplace and the boy playing with a ball. Robyn's words were consistent and compatible with her earlier conversation.

Robyn said that Helen, the ghost, likes to be around people. She said the little boy bounced the ball, then stopped, and when Robyn asked him to bounce it again, he did.

Robyn went into detail about her life in New Orleans. One night her sister sat up in bed, eyes open, chatting with someone (who was not there). Robyn talked about growing up in New Orleans and her ninety-seven-year-old mother.

During the holiday season, the ghost Helen has been seen, heard and acted out in the bar of the Newes. One might say the spirits are unbelievable. *Photo by Joyce Dresser.*

From her mother, Robyn believes that when someone talks to her in her dreams, it is an indication a person is about to die. The dream is a portent of things to come and prepares the recipient for the impending death of a relative or an acquaintance.

I spoke briefly with our hostess, Esther. She was bubbly and said she lived upstairs. I gave her my card and asked her to tell me what she had experienced.

Early in the new year, I sat down with another waitress, Jackie, whom I'd met briefly on a previous visit. Jackie has worked at the Newes for two years and experienced what Adrianne said about the bouncing Christmas ornament.

She also was on site the night when wine glasses leapt off the bar, smashing on the floor. She confirmed that Carrie was present when that occurred. Evidently, the jumping glasses has happened more than once.

Jackie said the ghost Helen is not around in the summer; she's strictly an off-season phenomenon. And Helen wants to be noticed, which explains her aberrant, but social, behavior.

While Jackie said she's not fearful to be working at the Newes, she does not enjoy going through paperwork in an upstairs office alone and away from other people. The solitude gives her a creepy feeling.

One more Kelley House employee I had to meet was Esther. According to Jackie, "Esther's used to the activity." Sounded like she's worth talking to.

WE INTERRUPT OUR TALE to note the story we are about to relate has already made the rounds on social media. However, it most certainly bears retelling:

> *Some guests of the hotel claim that there may be other guests staying there who aren't exactly still alive. From a dead sailor taking a shower in a maid's quarters to guests hearing what sounds like furniture being rearranged, the hotel seemed to be a hot spot for paranormal activity.*[6]

Esther works the evening shift at the Newes. I had to stop by the Newes, not for another ghostly interview, but because I'd left my credit card there the day before. We met by chance outside, and Esther hugged both Joyce and me. I sat down with Esther to hear her tale.

"Esther," I said. "We met you a month ago. You have a ghost story?"

She smiled, "Yes, I do. I have quite a tale to tell."

Esther has lived upstairs in the Kelley House for twenty years. Back in 2004, she had an experience that she cannot erase from her mind.

Esther was in her room, and a man came in through the door. He was a bald white man. He passed by her and went into the bathroom. Esther heard the water turn on in the shower. He took a shower; then he left. When he was gone, she found sand on the floor by the shower.

Another girl across the hall also saw him.

While shocked and startled by this experience, Esther was neither frightened nor fearful. And she continued to live and work in the building, which says a lot.

Esther had another experience while lying on her bed in her room one night, watching television. The remote control was nowhere near her. Suddenly, the television started to change channels. It went back and forth.

"There is a real ghost in the Kelley House," said Esther. "The ghost we call Helen is by the fireplace in the Newes. And one time a guest saw a man standing by the front door of the pub. The man just disappeared."

Esther paused, then repeated herself: "They are real ghosts. They are friendly. We feel their presence. You know about the glasses that slide off the table." Esther went on, talking about Helen: "She's here in the winter, but not the summer." She talked about the whaling men who went off to sea and how many of them died. She thinks Helen is a widow. "She always comes back in the winter." Esther is not scared; she feels comfortable around these ghosts in the Kelley House.

WE SCANNED TRIP ADVISOR and got a taste of what happened to one hotel guest:

> I had an encounter with a ghost named Helen who, we were told, died on the 3rd floor. We were also told that she mostly appears to men but she appeared to me, a woman. It was horrific. Don't believe me?…Ask management. They gave us lunch at their nearby pub to attempt to compensate and changed our room to the first floor. I would never stay there again. It took me a long time to get over the experience.…If I have!

*Date of stay: October 2014*
*Room tip: Not on the third floor with Helen!*
*Trip type: Traveled as a couple*
*Duxbury, MA, reviewed September 21, 2015; date of stay October 2014*

SOME PEOPLE ARE NOT believers. Others are curious. If we want to explore the supernatural, what better way than to engage a paranormal team to investigate?

Such a team was employed to investigate the Kelley House and came up with a finding:

> *The verdict? Some ghosts were still lingering on the premises, not all of them bad, some friendly who were just hanging out. Whether you believe or not, there are hotel staff members who will tell you all kinds of stories about the haunted adjoining rooms, 305 and 307![7]*

Now, about that paranormal team. The Vineyard's premier ghost hunter, Holly Nadler, submitted an account of what happened when ghost busters came to the Kelley House back in 2014. Some twenty-five guests were invited to visit the Kelley House on North Water Street. They were ushered into adjoining rooms, 305 and 307, supposedly the home to many occult experiences.

We checked in with Mary Elizabeth Surprenant, who lives in Oak Bluffs and was part of the investigation at the Kelley House. The event primarily took place in a conference room adjacent to the Newes, where the group had lunch. They toured upstairs in the Kelley House, rooms 305 and 307. The whole-day event took place in January, and it was very windy and cold.

Everyone took the investigation seriously:

> *The only issue I had was there were quite a few people there, so noise contamination was confounding the experience. We couldn't hear very well with rattling windows and a lot of people who wanted to talk. I had a recorder but didn't pick up anything unusual. It was my first time to be part of a ghost hunting experience. It was fun, overall.*

The leaders of the ghost hunters were people with a common goal who hailed from various points in Massachusetts, Rhode Island and New Jersey. Tiffany Rice, a spiritual medium, was part of the program. Tiffany did get some messages from people who had passed on.

Mary Surprenant said, "I remember a brief, fleeting seemingly phantom smell." She clarified, "I definitely smelled perfume, but it was hard to tell where it originated. It was not from our group because I would have detected it earlier. It was a fleeting aroma, and it disappeared."

For the past ten years, Mary has been interested in ghosts; she and her friend Ellen have participated in a number of Rhode Island paraconferences. She said, "My experience at the Paine House in Coventry, Rhode Island, is special. I've been there three times. We have a small, respectful group. It's very quiet. The house is very active; it's a very old building."

At the Paine House, "Ellen and I were sitting on the floor and we distinctly heard and felt a tapping sound. It was like a ball bouncing. We felt the bounce with our hands as we were sitting on the floor. We noted the vibration, then it stopped. It was an unsettling experience, but not frightening." Sounds very similar to what Robyn experienced.

At the Paine House, a little girl has frequently been seen in the dining room, next to the mudroom. Mary and Ellen were on the second floor. "We were ready to go downstairs. I looked down and saw a white light by the steps, just at the height of a child's head. Gradually, it disappeared."

Former parking clerk Donna Michalski of Oak Bluffs remarked on how the evening turned into the classic dark and stormy night as wind gusted under the eaves of the Courthouse. This was fine for creating horror-style atmospherics, but it played havoc with the team's attempt to pick up unusual transmissions on the EVP recordings. Michalski said, "I kept hearing them muttering, 'That damn wind!'"

Another participant, Tiffany Rice, was present. Rice made a later appearance in rooms 305 and 307. She confirmed that any number of spirits were present and accounted for. Interestingly, she, too received the impression of a little girl bathing.

Holly Nadler concluded her commentary: "Clearly a good time was had by all, and a visit to the Kelley House for food and spirits—both alcoholic and occult—are continually on tap."[8]

Another person shared her experience with the supernatural. Stephanie Barnhart described visiting what likely was the Courthouse, a separate building, run by the Kelley House, back in 2013. Her blog begins with a description of the cottage she stayed in with her girlfriend:

> It had the customary white-picket front porch, and the old musty smell when you walk in. The bedrooms were on the bottom, and the staircase swirled around to a kitchen up top, and open living room that had a patio deck. ADORABLE. Until 4 am.

She set the stage:

> It is eerily quiet in Martha at night. Dead silence. So when I heard the first noise that woke me up, I figured it was just because of the silence, I could hear anything. Then it happened again—it literally sounded like someone was moving the kitchen chairs around upstairs—just like someone was pulling it out to sit in it, and then get up, and push it back. W.T.F. It did this about 4 different times or at least at that point my heart was beating so loud it drowned out anything else. I was so scared I couldn't sleep. I was TRYING to not hear it but my adrenaline was pumping and ANY little sound was setting me off. Needless to say I didn't get much sleep and woke up looking like this…

Judging from Stephanie's perspective, the hotel is pretty big, with smaller cottages nearby. "It also has this creepy, never-updated bar in the far back bottom of the hotel." We know that as the Newes from America.

The following evening, Stephanie wasted no time:

> I asked the bartender straight up—"Tell me the truth—this place is haunted isn't it." Now, being that we're tourists I figured he'd shrug his shoulders, kick around some dirt on the floor and then rush over to help other patrons. Instead—he quickly added, "Of course it is! Everything on this island is haunted! You want to hear some real stories? let me get some of the maids that live here all year …"

She goes on.

> My mouth dropped. Lydia [Stephanie's girlfriend] was laughing. Maybe we shouldn't have been strolling in the local cemetery the moment

*we got into the island. Then this maid came over and told us how a sailor comes and showers in her quarters.*

And the story continues:

*She said the FIRST TIME she saw a man walking out of her bathroom and it freaked her out. There was even water AND sand in the shower like someone had just used it. She mentioned this to the management and they said—oh, that's just one of the sailors that used to live here. He's a nice ghost.*

That night, Stephanie experienced the strange sounds again, at 4:00 a.m. Chairs were pushed across the floor upstairs. Stephanie's roommate did not wake up. No confirmation, but Stephanie knew what she heard.

*Why was I the only one hearing it? Was it REAL?? It moved again. I was pinned with fear. This HAD to be real. THERE WAS SOMETHING UPSTAIRS. So what does one do when having a paranormal experience? Ride it out. I mean, what was I supposed to do? Run outside and see MORE ghosts? It was the WORST TWO NIGHTS OF MY LIFE.*[9]

We cannot add to Stephanie's tale; she says it all.

# 3

# UPPER MAIN STREET

*Is there a ghost at the county jail?*

So begins a tale that has seeped beneath the eighteen-inch granite walls and betwixt steel-barred windows of the Dukes County House of Correction on Upper Main Street, Edgartown.

The jail is situated on the former site of Dr. Fisher's Fort, the storage area for barrels of whale oil awaiting distribution. Dr. Fisher (1800–1876) was the premier financier of the whaling industry on Martha's Vineyard. Besides overseeing the purchase, sale and distribution of whale oil, Fisher operated a spermaceti candle factory and a hardtack bakery. Perhaps Old Joe, as the ghost of the jail is known, is a recalcitrant whaleman, hanging around to be part of the action. Or maybe Old Joe, as some say, is a criminal, still serving his sentence in the afterlife.

In any case, several correction officers were interviewed regarding the jailhouse ghost. We share some of comments as reported in the *Vineyard Gazette* from thirty years ago.

Sergeant Randolph Ditson was quoted as saying, "I didn't really believe it when I started here." Once Sergeant Ditson learned about the ghost, he admitted to being slightly dismayed. After more than eight years, mostly on the graveyard shift, Ditson accepted the spectral apparition, neither inmate nor officer, but a presence in the old part of the Big House.

"You walk upstairs and then all of a sudden you feel it is real cool," Sergeant Ditson reported. On the ground floor, he said, he has been sitting

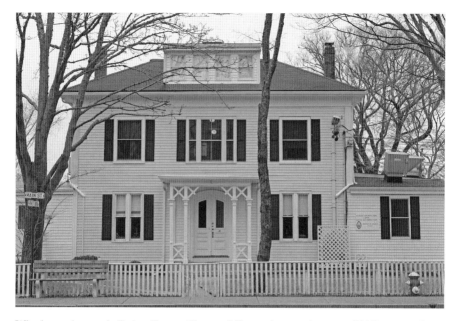

Who knew the stately Dukes County House of Correction was home to Old Joe, a warden who still patrols the cells? *Photo by Joyce Dresser.*

at his desk and heard the water turned on in the kitchen. He has walked into the kitchen to find no one there to turn the water on. At other times, the ghost has played with the lights. The ghost has been known to operate the typewriter and turn the radio on. "One night we heard typing, and there was nobody in there typing," Ditson said. "He is a harmless spirit that just likes to be around."

Another corrections officer, William Searle, considered Old Joe an inmate or resident of the building. Searle said there was no routine or schedule to hear Old Joe; every so often he would make his presence known.

"The midnight shift was a good time to do paperwork, so you would spend hours at a desk," Searle recalled. Then, upstairs, he began hearing someone moving down the hall. It didn't make sense. All the inmates were supposedly locked in their cells and asleep. "I heard distinct footsteps. I cannot tell you how many times it happened. It got to a point I'd hear him walking around quite a lot. At first I thought that an inmate got out of his cell. I would go through the whole institution with the lights on and then I'd find no one," Searle said.

The footsteps in the hallway upstairs changed to footsteps on the wooden stairs. "Then I would hear footsteps walking the full length of the ground

Step into the Dukes County Jail and hear from the wardens who have an extra hand on duty. *Courtesy of Mark Lovewell and the* Vineyard Gazette.

floor hall to the office. And then I would turn around fully expecting to see someone and there would be no one," Searle recalled.[10]

The jail has a number of television screens to monitor activity. Officer Robert Duart had heard stories of the ghost at the County Jail but never took the tales seriously. That is, he didn't believe until one night he and a couple of other officers were monitoring the screen focused on the inmates' day room. There on the screen was a blurry creature stealthily easing itself across the screen. That sense of someone or something else being around was very evident.

Jail records indicate an inmate named Joe hanged himself on site in 1950. Maybe he returns to keep an eye on the facility. Sheriff Chris Look heard stories that the ghost of Fred Worden, a former jail warden, still made his rounds. No one knows for sure what Old Joe is up to, but the stories linger.

We checked in with Mark Lovewell, the reporter/photographer who researched and wrote the story of Old Joe. He vividly remembered the piece. "I loved writing that story. It was so much fun…great to uncover something for Halloween which was at the time a fresh Vineyard story." He added that a number of people helped him with the story, people on the outside, as well as inside the Dukes County House of Correction. It's quite a tale.

RICHIE AND MISSY SMITH vividly remember their honeymoon on Martha's Vineyard over the Fourth of July weekend of 2000.

The couple lived in Charlottesville, Virginia, in 1998, and each noticed things that were not quite right but didn't talk about them. For example, the Elmo doll would go to sleep and snore on its own. Champagne flutes felt heavier than they should. Both Richie and Missy had the distinct impression, at various times, that someone was watching them. The final event was an incident in the carport, when Richie smashed the front of his car. They agree that accident was a deciding factor in why they moved to Martha's Vineyard, because Richie felt it was caused by something beyond him.

Richie and Missy celebrated their honeymoon by booking themselves at the Victorian Inn (now the Christopher) on South Water Street for three nights.

The couple is rigid in their housekeeping regimen, making their bed as soon as they are up, hanging their towels neatly in the bathroom and checking that the door is locked multiple times before leaving. Richie acknowledged he is obsessive-compulsive. Both he and Missy appreciate a tidy environment. Missy is a keen observer of detail; she knows when something is askew.

Their room at the Victorian Inn was on the third floor, farthest to the left when facing the inn from the street. When they went out for a walk, they closed the French door to the deck; when they returned, the door had opened on its own. They investigated, to see if someone could have opened the door from outside. Neither possible nor plausible.

Their towels were on the floor—not like they fell—it was as if they were dropped there, intentionally. The Smiths checked with housekeeping to see if anyone had been in their room. The housekeepers had not.

The rug under the four-poster bed was moved. Now that was strange because the bed was literally sitting on the rug, which was on wall-to-wall

Ghostly tales abound around the Victorian Inn (now The Christopher), from shifting rugs to past miscreants. *Photo by Joyce Dresser.*

carpeting. More than once they noticed the rug in a different location under the bed. A pitcher with flowers had been moved about. They specifically set something out, and it was moved when they returned.

Richie and Missy asked each other what happened. It felt odd to them. They were not frightened, but it was an uncomfortable feeling. As noted, this happened more than twenty years ago, yet it is seared in their memory.

SOMETIMES, THINGS JUST HAPPEN. I got word that Greer Thornton, proprietor of Atria, an upper Main Street restaurant, had a few ghost stories to share. So I met with Greer at the Y after our workout.

Greer has had three encounters with a force or power or energy over the past twenty years. In 2001, shortly after Greer and her husband assumed management of Atria, Greer was at the front desk, going over paperwork.

It was one or two o'clock in the morning. It was quiet, and she was the only one in the facility.

While she was busy reviewing names and numbers, she experienced a clear voice from inside her ear. It was like a whisper, and it just said her name, "Greer." She was startled but unafraid and actually appreciated being recognized.

In 2007, it was off-season and Atria was closed for the winter. Greer had to go into the restaurant late in the day. She brought her two Labs with her. They went into the building, but the dogs stopped short, soon after they entered. Greer was heading to the kitchen. The dogs refused to follow.

Greer opened the door to the kitchen and was greeted with long, loud screams. There was no one there, but the sound was deafening. Greer got what she needed and left the kitchen. She had to return a few minutes later, and the screams erupted again. No one was in the kitchen, but the sound was deafening.

The third incident occurred a couple of years ago, in 2018. Again, Greer was in the building. Another employee was upstairs in the office, and

The owner of Atria, Greer Thornton, offers a clear and concise description of three incidents that fit into our ghostly theme. *Photo by Thomas Dresser.*

there were people working in the kitchen. Greer left her office and looked downstairs. She caught a glimpse of something passing through; it was a person, ephemeral, in an undefined greenish/gray outfit. Greer isn't sure if it was a man or a woman but leans toward a man. He just moved across the lobby and disappeared. That was it.

Greer has considered why these incidents occurred. With the first one, when her name was spoken, she felt that was a welcome call, as she and her husband had recently purchased the restaurant. On the second one, with the screams, it could be that the spirits of Atria were upset that the restaurant was not open in the off-season. And for the third, the visitation by someone or something, Greer is unsure what prompted or caused that event.

One visitor whom Greer is happy to acknowledge was a few years ago when President Obama enjoyed dinner at Atria. Of all her stories, we're sure that is Greer's favorite.

~

LIZ VILLARD AND I enjoyed lunch at the Kelley House one day to chat about her connections with Edgartown. Liz is a cemetery maven who has offered ghost tours. She worked as a docent at the Vincent House, one of the oldest houses on the island. Liz has a background in theater and explained that many people want to hear of ghosts and scandal, whereas her focus is on the historical background of various sites. "My ghost stories are historical," she says. "I don't do scary things."

As her knowledge expanded, so did her reputation. Liz was invited to participate in a radio program, *The Point*, with Mark Jasper, sharing ghost stories. One of the tales was about a chambermaid who worked at the Edgartown Inn. Jasper, author of *Haunted Cape Cod and the Islands*, described the maid, who loved her work but was forced to retire due to her age. She died and was seen in several spectral sightings, apparently unwilling to go quietly into the unknown.

Liz also spoke briefly about Jasper's interview with George, an employee of the Daggett House who had seen a ghost several times both at the Daggett House and at his own home. Liz was intrigued that Jasper's recorder jammed when he tried to record the interview.

"I have my doubts about the Daggett House," says Liz. She discounts the story of the two brothers and hidden dog as a fable. Both boys knew

The old Coffin house, built in 1703, has a single ghostly sighting, dating back nearly a century. One is enough, right? *Photo by Joyce Dresser.*

about the secret staircase; how could the dog not bark and not have others look for him there? Yet Liz acknowledges that "people want more." There is curiosity and intrigue about ghost stories from young and old alike. The unexplained is exciting.

That said, Liz agreed, "I believe there are forces that turn up." She cannot explain all the sightings by the employee named George. Yet she's torn: "If people see a ghost, I don't really buy into it."

We spoke of the Coffin House on North Water Street, managed by The Trust. The house played a role in the whaling history of Edgartown and was built in 1703 by John Coffin, a transplanted Nantucketeer who came to work on the Vineyard as a blacksmith.

Grace Coffin lived in the house with her new husband, Dr. Daniel Fisher, until their house on Main Street was built. Liz pointed out that the front entryway of the Fisher House mirrors that of the Coffin House; the good doctor copied the old house.

Marge Willoughby knows the Coffin House inside and out and spent a lot of time in the attic. She's sorry to report, "No sightings on my part." However, she added when her late father-in-law "played baseball out back with Bob Carroll as a kid, he said they would sometimes see the ghost in the window. I think the building was empty at that time but not sure and no explanation I can remember about the so-called ghost."

So there's a bit of a ghost connected with the Coffin House.

We moved on to the Vincent House, which has a reputation for ghosts.

The Vincent House was built in Katama in 1672, and today it stands as one of the oldest existing houses on Martha's Vineyard. It was used as a fishing camp in Katama in the early twentieth century. In 1945, John MacKenty bought the house and maintained it as a structure from its initial historic period. It was not renovated but preserved as a structure with the atmosphere and ambiance of four centuries of Vineyard history. The house was moved into Edgartown in 1977 and managed by the Vineyard Trust, formerly the Preservation Trust.

The Trust opened the Vincent House for tourists to learn about Vineyard life over the past three hundred–plus years. Employees worked out of a back room on the first floor. Liz Villard worked as a docent and often left the door open to allow fresh air to permeate the ancient structure. At times, the door would shut abruptly, apparently on its own, with neither a person nor a gust of wind to make it move.

Shortly before Liz became the tour guide, there was a robbery at the Vincent House, and arrowheads and points were stolen. The Trust installed a security alarm system. On occasion, the alarm system would go off, unexpectedly, without reason—it just went off. The Trust found it very irritating. "We put a Christmas tree up in the Victorian room, a nineteenth-century room in the house, and the alarm went off." Liz observed that it was as if the previous owner did not want any changes to the house, and said, "We can take care of our house; leave us alone."

Liz added a twist of spectral supposition to the story: "A woman's ghost appeared to two junior volunteers (sixth and seventh graders). They saw her in the blue nineteenth-century room. They were so freaked that they refused to go back in the house. One of them drew a picture of her that got the shape of the skirt right for the period of the blue room."

Even having experienced seeing that apparition, the junior volunteers thought it would be fun to sleep in the house on Halloween. "The junior

The Vincent House, built in 1672, bears more than island artifacts in its historical array. *Photo by Joyce Dresser.*

volunteers also did sleep overnight in the house. Two of their friends turned up and pretended to be ghosts and scared everyone, even me."

Liz feels the Vincent House got more friendly over "the ten years I gave to the town." Previously, there had been a cold atmosphere to the house.

She said some people get emotional about their ghostly feelings. Many people want to see ghosts in graveyards and older haunted houses. It's part of the allure of haunted happenings.

THE SHIVERICK INN, 5 Peases Point Way, was the home of a very respected physician. According to its website, the Shiverick was built in 1840 for Dr. Clement Francis Shiverick, the town doctor. "The Shiverick Inn today offers a delightful blend of past and present." The site notes, "Great care was taken in its recent restoration to preserve the architectural details of this gracious mansion, revive its romantic ambiance and exquisitely recreate its elegant grandeur."

Karen Coffey, a Vineyard Haven paranormal, knew people who used to live there. "There was all kinds of energy in that house. You felt a cat brushing up on your leg. There were cold rooms. Doors would open and close randomly."

As an experienced paranormal, Karen says, "Every old house has a ghost; only particular people can sense them."

I ASKED LIZA WILLIAMSON of the Dukes County Courthouse if she was ever fearful when working at the courthouse, frightened by a ghost or a spectral image or sound or presence she couldn't explain.

Liza said she's worked on stormy days when the wind is blowing and the windows rattle. She looked around and saw and felt nothing. She has been working at the courthouse for many years and never experienced any unusual or unexplained sound or sensed anything out of the ordinary.

Her words mirror what Joe Sollitto said after his forty-plus years working at the courthouse. No ghosts. No goblins. Nothing to be afraid of. Like Liza, Joe spent some late hours alone in the courthouse and never felt a sense of

While rich in island history, the Dukes County Courthouse lays claim to no spectral sightings, whether during a midnight assignment or a daytime murder trial. *Photo by Joyce Dresser.*

doubt or fear. He is an honest soul, and I believe he has not encountered anything in the area of haunted happenings within the confines of the courthouse.

Of course, both Liza and Joe are only two employees of the courthouse, but their spectrum of people who work there is broad. Neither had heard any rumors or any fears about any ghostly experiences, and I take them at their word.

# 4

# WEST TISBURY

North Tisbury is clearly and unmistakably *south* of Tisbury,"[11] an anomaly that begs explanation.

Tisbury and Edgartown were both incorporated on July 8, 1671. (The third township, Chilmark, was incorporated on September 14, 1694.) For two centuries, the township of Tisbury included a number of little villages, including Holmes Hole and West Chop, the harbor, the Lagoon, North Tisbury, Christiantown, Deep Bottom, Cape Higgon and present-day West Tisbury.

People in the original center of the town of Tisbury used the land and streams for their economic livelihood; mills and farms dominated. Holmes Hole was a small village where people profited from harbor activities. Tisbury was Congregationalist; Holmes Hole tended toward Baptist and Methodist faiths.

The village of North Tisbury is centered by the great white oak at the intersection of North and State Roads. Today, Glassworks, State Road Restaurant and Middletown Nursery are the primary businesses.

In the 1860s the village of Tisbury began to refer to itself as West Tisbury. By 1892, West Tisbury had split from Holmes Hole so each could retain its identity. The village of Holmes Hole was renamed Tisbury; the village by the harbor was called Vineyard Haven. Thus North Tisbury came to be south of Tisbury. And so it was that the one town became two.

On another note, there is a stone marker in the State Forest where four towns meet, known as the Four Town Bound: Oak Bluffs, Tisbury, West Tisbury and Edgartown converge at this point.

ON A BRISK FEBRUARY morning, three dozen hardy souls set off on a walk along an Ancient Way in Tisbury. The goal was to explore the environs of Redcoat Hill, a hummock nestled in the woods off State Road. The old roadway edged signs of development, burrowed deep in the scrub oak, then gradually rose in a majestically carved arcing roadway along Redcoat Hill.

In our modern world, we rarely consider an invasion of enemy forces in our homeland. During the Second World War, we feared Nazi planes in the air and submarines in our waters. The only invasion of the Vineyard during the Second World War was conducted by American soldiers perfecting tactics to use overseas. They approached from Camp Edwards, on the Cape, and launched a practice attack on the Vineyard. Thus the only invaders have been fellow Americans, preparing for the real thing: the invasion of Normandy in 1944.

British redcoats on Martha's Vineyard? Are we talking changing of the guard or ghostly spirits from long ago? *Photo by Joyce Dresser.*

Other than the British, that is.

Redcoat Hill was a summit reportedly used by the British to view Holmes Hole Harbor during the raid by General Grey in 1778. "Red Coat Hill served as a lookout over the harbor during the Revolutionary War, but during a 1778 invasion known as Grey's Raid, Red Coats invaded the hill, leaving a garment behind."[12] (The area is forested today, so the harbor view is nonexistent.) Later, when a local Vineyarder stumbled upon the jacket, the appellation Redcoat Hill was attached to this part of the landscape.

General Sir Charles Grey commanded the captains of a fleet of warships and transport vessels who scavenged the New England coast, reaching Holmes Hole on September 10. "The sight must have been a thrilling one—two score vessels including twelve ships of the line. It amazed and terrified the peaceful people."[13]

Grey proposed not to harm any Vineyarders provided the local farmers march their sheep and cattle down island to the British ships in the harbor. The sheep would be used to feed the redcoats who planned to winter in New York. More than four thousand redcoats intimidated any Vineyarder who refused to comply.

On September 11, the warship *Scorpion* sailed to Edgartown and destroyed ships in the harbor, while the Forty-Fourth Regiment marched by land, seizing weapons en route. Down island, redcoats disabled the vital saltworks, stole armaments and destroyed Vineyard vessels. There were no Vineyard casualties.

"A detachment of 450 troops, a tiny fraction of Grey's force, but more than enough to outnumber the local militia, went ashore to maintain order and assure compliance."[14] Redcoats marched up island to North Tisbury and Chilmark.

Remaining troops "landed at the head of Vineyard Haven harbor, and camped on the open field now traversed by Main street, and north of Church street. It was the first close view of British 'regulars' which the Vineyarders had obtained since the war opened."[15]

British soldiers camped out in Vineyard Haven, many in tents along Church Street. They maintained a fortified camp on what was known as Manter Hill (up Church Street), and "when the troops broke camp here and re-embarked from the beach below, it was the last time the soil of Massachusetts was pressed by the foot of a British soldier."[16]

The siege lasted until September 14, when the sheep-laden ships departed for New York. There the British wintered, dining on Vineyard sheep.

THE SON OF CAPTAIN Myles Standish built a house in West Tisbury in 1667. The Josiah Standish House sits on the cusp of Brandy Brow in West Tisbury overlooking Parsonage Pond. It functioned as a bed-and-breakfast in the 1990s.

Tara Whiting-Wells moved back to the Vineyard in 1993 and lived at the Standish house, her family's home. She recalled there was a door between two bedrooms that would not open. The house had settled, and the door was stuck. One morning, the door was wide open. Who could have done that? And how?

Another incident occurred that gave Tara pause. She was asleep one night when she heard footsteps on the metal grate outside her bedroom. Her dog

Uninvited guests partied well into the night at the Standish homestead, built in 1667 by Josiah Standish (1633–1690) son of Myles Standish, military advisor to the Pilgrims at Plimoth Plantation. *Photo by Thomas Dresser.*

began to bark. She tried to ignore the sound and go back to sleep, but she heard the footsteps again reverberate on the register by her door. It was an unsettling experience, but she handled it well.

Neither the open door nor the footsteps frightened Tara. She felt comfortable in the old house, familiar in the surroundings and unafraid.

In the mid-1990s, Tara was staying at the house. One night, a guest had an experience he shared with Tara that she cannot explain—but she believes every word.

In the middle of the night, the guest got up to use the bathroom. He had to walk through the dining room. The guest glanced into the living room and was startled by what he saw.

Men wearing bright red jackets were gathered in the living room, laughing and chatting with one another. Women were there too, attired in period dress. They were enjoying a social time together, drinking and savoring the atmosphere.

The redcoats took no notice of the guest passing by their frivolity. The company acted quite at home in their setting, with no intention to calm down or quiet their revelry.

Next morning, the guest asked Tara Whiting-Welles if there had been a play the night before. Was the cast party held at the bed-and-breakfast?

No play. No cast party. Apparently, a company of British redcoats had gathered in the Standish house that evening. What better place for soldiers to gather for a boisterous evening of fun and frivolity? Yet that was more than two centuries after the British were on island. It seems the guest at the bed-and-breakfast encountered uninvited guests who returned to the premises.

Several people corroborated this ghostly experience. We confirmed the story with Tara Whiting-Wells, and her uncle, Allen Whiting, recounted it for the press in 2017: Mr. Whiting related a secondhand account from his niece, who stayed at the house years ago with her family. Her former father-in-law was asleep in a guest bedroom, and he claimed he woke up, opened the door to the dining room and saw a group of British soldiers wearing red coats and dancing.[17]

Tales of the Revolution were shared by Charles Hine in his little book of unusual Vineyard experiences, compiled and published in 1908. "Tradition says that when the island was raided by Grey, part of the cellar under this [unspecified] dwelling was hastily walled off, thus secreting a quantity of powder, guns, and possibly valuables."[18] While the redcoats camped nearby, no one suspected the interior wall.

We share a memorable tale of bravery and deception by Captain Nathan Smith of Makonikey. During Grey's Raid, British soldiers were on the beach gathering local cattle. Captain Smith marched back and forth on the shore, shouting orders, leading his imaginary troops back and forth, barking commands hidden by a sand dune. He ordered his nonexistent forces to prepare to fire, which precipitated a dramatic rush for the boats by the fearful British. It does make a great visual of the daring character of Nathan Smith.

A local boy, William Downs, went hunting in Mink Meadows and shot a number of teal, or duck. On his way home, he was accosted by a British officer who demanded why the boy had a gun. The lad claimed he was hunting food for his family and sold a duck to the redcoat.

During mealtime one night, while wintering at Valley Forge, where starvation competed with the cold in bringing Washington's army nearly to its knees, a Vineyarder, one Abner Luce, was outraged when an officer sought to take his food from him. The officer wanted to punish young Luce, but his commanding officer agreed with Luce, arguing that any soldier who failed to stand up for his grub would not be a good soldier.

Just beyond Hazzleton's Head, a bluff on West Chop, near Frog Alley, Vineyard Haven, was "a house of mystery, whose shuttered windows no longer search the horizon. Here lived one Daggett, a Tory, on the very edge of the bluff."[19] Daggett was a Vineyarder but served as a spy for the British, a friend to our enemy. When local colonists discovered Daggett's deceit, they marched down, surrounded Daggett's house and seized two British soldiers as prisoners; the soldiers were later exchanged for a captured colonist.

And it was during Grey's Raid that British redcoats diligently sought buried treasure. While there is no record they found anything of note, more recent treasure-hunters, armed with metal detectors, have uncovered Spanish coins, which could have been dropped by the British troops.

FARTHER NORTH ALONG STATE Road, in North Tisbury, stands the majestic great white oak, known as a wolf, as it's the only tree of its kind in the field. Years ago, a young girl walked beneath its branches that now arch along the ground. The little girl crossed State Road to the large house to play cribbage with Bert Humphrey, who lived in the old Humphrey house next to Humphrey's Bakery. The Humphrey house sits back from the road by the intersection of North and State Roads, across from Priester's Pond.

Instead of knocking at the side door, as she was told, the little girl approached the front door. She looked in the window. In the front parlor, near the door, was a rocking chair. And the rocking chair was visibly rocking back and forth. No one was in the chair; no one was even in the room. Why was it rocking? How was it rocking?

Jim Powell's sister-in-law Sheila Humphrey has seen the rocking chair rocking with no one nearby. Once, while she was living there, she was watching television; she turned around, and the chair was rocking. This mysterious rocking chair has to be seen to be believed.

We STOPPED TO SEE Donna Humphrey at her bakery, Life at Humphrey's, at the Woodland strip mall in Vineyard Haven.

"Could I ask you a question?"

"Of course," she smiled.

"What do you know about a rocking chair at the old house on State Road?"

Donna nodded. The rocking chair just rocks, all by itself. Without hesitation, she confirmed the self-rocking chair, then launched into a number of intriguing details about haunted happenings of the old Humphrey house, built in the 1870s, at the intersection of North and State Roads in North Tisbury.

Yes, the rocking chair rocks by itself. People have seen it. Even when someone is in the room, the chair starts rocking. By itself. No one can explain it. It happens. And there are other haunted happenings.

Donna's grandparents used to have a butler who worked for them at their home in Cambridge as well as their summer house in West Tisbury. His name was Dan Baxter. Baxter often wore a top hat, and sometimes tails, when he worked for the couple. He was a loyal employee who treated the Humphreys with courtesy and respect. Baxter died in the Humphrey homestead years ago.

When Donna was eight years old, she slept over at her grandparents' house. One day, she was with her grandmother in the kitchen, and she saw the butler, complete with his top hat. He had a tray in hand, just holding it

Donna Humphrey, whose grandparents lived in this house, saw the ghost of Dan Baxter, their deceased butler, attired in top hat and tails, with a tray in hand. Honest. *Photo by Joyce Dresser.*

out for her. Donna was surprised and turned to tell her grandmother. When she looked back, Baxter had disappeared.

Years later, Donna and her cousins were talking about the butler. It turns out all the relatives knew about him; it was common knowledge in the family. The teenagers got out a Ouija board to try to contact him. That was when Donna asked her grandmother: "Why didn't you tell me about the butler?"

Donna's mother believes Donna did see Baxter. She believes because she is familiar with unusual experiences in the old Humphrey house. She has heard noises that cannot be explained; they are not footsteps but the noise of movement. She has smelled strange aromas that she cannot pinpoint. And she had a very strange experience when she went upstairs and down the hall to one of the bedrooms. She stood in the doorway, and the room was filled with fog. As she looked at the window, there was a light in the glass. And then it all disappeared.

These tales are part of family legend; family members firmly believe the house is haunted, not in a fearful, frightening way, but that there is a presence, a ghost, a sense that someone or something was in the house with the family.

Jim Powell is a Vineyarder. His mother grew up on island and shared her memories as a teenager coming of age during World War II. Jim has been a teacher, a realtor, a man of many vocations, interests and abilities. He shared some spectral memories.

People in North Tisbury have been awakened in the middle of the night by a dog barking ferociously. The dog owners have seen their dog barking at a shadow on the walkway. However, there is no one casting a shadow. There is no one around. It is a vision. The dog continues to bark at the shadow, but no one is there. Apparently, the dog senses the presence of someone or something and barks at it.

A whaling captain's house in North Tisbury was home for a little boy aged three or four. His family noticed he was engaged in talking and playing with another little boy. The second boy was not real, yet he was naked and was seen to run through the house and upstairs. He was not a member of the family, and no one knew who he was. Family members who followed this stranger upstairs found no one. There was no explanation for this unusual apparition.

BEFORE CEMETERIES CAME INTO vogue on the Vineyard, when a family member passed on, the body was buried on the grounds, in the backyard. Some people claim apparitions are connected to these burials, that the dead still have something they want to contribute to the current situation.

A number of people have requested Jim Powell come to their house, as they believe there is "an unwanted visitor in the house." He has gone to the house in question after hearing about these eyewitness accounts from homeowners in West Tisbury. Jim said he acts almost as a minister. "I encourage the entity to move on. I talk with them. It's like an exorcism. I come in and pray. They seem to have a visitor in their house, but they don't want them."

Jim continued. One story involved a little boy in a bedroom. The homeowner saw the little boy and asked Jim to intervene: "We wonder if you could pray and get him to leave." Jim said, "I do what they ask. It's low key and seems to work."

Jim Powell added, "I connect with history. I was part of the State Historical Board, the museum board. I can comfort people, like at a funeral." In addition, "all these North Tisbury ghosts seemed to have a message or experience to share, warn or comfort their living family members with. It wasn't just random or for entertainment nor for haunting. None of them were for haunting."

It seems that Jim has a knack for helping people move along, assisting them with coming to grips with death. And he looks at things from a historical perspective.

NORTH TISBURY BURIAL GROUND, aka the Middletown Cemetery is located on Rogers Path, in the shadow of the great white oak at the intersection of State Road and North Road. The cemetery has ninety-four graves and has been closed to new interments since 1960.

One of the more specific spectral sightings on the Vineyard occurred near the North Tisbury Burial Ground on Rogers Path on New Year's Eve 1914.

Who would guess a spirit would surface in this peaceful little cemetery along Rogers Path in West Tisbury? *Photo by Thomas Dresser.*

According to the *Boston Globe*, a local woman, Rebecca Wagner of North Tisbury, noticed, "An oval light hung just above the ground among the gravestones. It was very white and bright. The light rose and tumbled over, like a flame, or a miniature geyser of fireworks." Wagner and her neighbor watched the light for half an hour and claimed it was so bright they could make out the letters on the gravestones.

This story was revisited by *Gazette* reporter Jim Hickey in 2007:

> *The next haunted locale on my itinerary was the West Tisbury cemetery, source of many a ghostly tale over the centuries. The most famous made it all the way to the front page of the Dec. 31, 1939 edition of the* Boston Globe *in a story that recounted ghosts had "broken the winter quiet that usually prevails over Middletown, the small hamlet on the Island of Martha's Vineyard." The story states that two women spotted a light floating in the cemetery so bright they could read the letters on the tombstones.*

As the reader appreciates the cemetery sighting, we understand how ghost stories preserve and protect and persevere in characterizing the mystery and excitement of the unknown. This simple tale, more than a century old, lingers in our collective memory, unexplained. It offers a spectral experience that continues to intrigue. That is the essence of a good ghost story. We believe, though we cannot quite understand how or why this unusual event occurred.

~

ON THE THEME OF sightings in a cemetery, Parson Thaxter, who fought at the Battle of Bunker Hill, saw a ghost in a Vineyard graveyard. E.T. Vincent's grandfather also saw this alleged ghost, a white figure meandering among the gravestones.

The ghost turned out to be a local woman wandering around in a bedsheet near the cemetery.

# 5

# OF MOSHUP AND MORE

In 1694, Chilmark became the third town to be incorporated on Martha's Vineyard. It comprised all the land in the southwest peninsula of Gay Head as well as Nomans Land. Legendary stories, old and new, have circulated over the years among the Wampanoag. We delve into the history of Native Americans on Martha's Vineyard, or Noepe, as it was known to them.

In the Wampanoag language, Noepe means "amid the waters," and that's how their story starts. Moshup was the legendary ancestor of Native Americans. He was a giant: bigger, stronger, smarter and more capable than any human. Native Americans refer to Moshup as their ancestor because he set in motion life on Martha's Vineyard for the Wampanoag tribe.

One of the earliest historical legends of Moshup is how he splashed through the shoreline of Cape Cod as he made his way to the Vineyard. Ocean water filled his giant footsteps as he plodded across the landscape, separating the Vineyard from the mainland. Thus was born Noepe, an island amid the waters.

The legend of Moshup explains how the Vineyard came to be separated from Cape Cod by his gigantic plodding footsteps parting the waters. Modern scientific studies attribute the geological formations to glacial activity. Great glaciers, some 1,500 feet high, sloughed down over the landscape from the north, gouging the ground like a slowly moving bulldozer. Eons later, during global warming, the glaciers melted, which caused ocean waters to rise.

Current estimates put the rise in water level at some four hundred feet—that's four hundred feet higher today than when the glaciers eased over the coastline six thousand years ago. Ocean waters rose and covered land, creating the islands of Martha's Vineyard and Nantucket.

Stories of Moshup abound. He wanted to teach his children, the Wampanoag, to hunt whale for food. Moshup stood high on the cliffs of Gay Head and dove down into the sea, swimming several miles into the ocean. There, he caught a whale by the tail and brought it ashore. He stood on the beach at Gay Head and swung the whale around and around his head, then crashed it against the cliffs. Blood from the whale turned the cliffs a deep, dark red.

Moshup brought his bride, Squant, and their dozen daughters to the shoreline to show them the import of hunting whales. "Standing at his door

The Gay Head shoreline is home to pirate tales and mysterious ocean experiences. *Photo by Joyce Dresser.*

67

he would catch a whale, or other great fish, by the tail and swing it up to his hearthstone where a fire always burned, constantly replenished by large forest trees which he pulled up by the roots for the purpose."[20]

To cook the whale, the Wampanoag cut down trees all across the peninsula of Gay Head and built fires to cook his whale. (According to legend, that is why there are no tall trees in Gay Head. Today we attribute the dearth of tall trees to the omnipresent salt air that continually wafts across the peninsula.) The Wampanoag cooked and ate the whale and learned how important it was to their well-being.

MOSHUP WAS FOOLED BY a woman on Cuttyhunk working in concert with the devil. However, the Wampanoag had no devil in their mythology; the devil was introduced by English theology in the early seventeenth century.

Moshup planned to build a bridge from Gay Head across the Sound to Cuttyhunk. He accepted a bet that he could build the bridge before the cock crowed to signify morning. He set to work. One version of the fable says a crab bit Moshup on his toe, and he had to halt his labors, so the bridge was never built. All that remains are the rocks he put in place.

A second story says that to prevent Moshup from winning his bet with the devil, a woman held a lantern to her rooster in the middle of the night. That inspired the cock to crow, thinking it was dawn. When the rooster crowed, Moshup lost his bet; thereafter the underwater rocks became known as Devil's Bridge.

Devil's Bridge represents a time when Moshup lost a bet. We recall the disaster off Martha's Vineyard in the winter of 1884, when the ship *City of Columbus* foundered on Devil's Bridge and 103 people met their death in the cold and stormy waters off Gay Head. The great glacial erratic still lies beneath the surface, a warning from Moshup when he lost his bet with the devil.

IN A 1955 PAGEANT about the history of the Wampanoag, Nanetta Madison said, "We with open ears know that the smoke stands as a sign of the undying love of Big Chief Moshup, the sign and seal of his love for us, his children.

And the faint sigh born on the wings of the wind, is Old Squant [his wife], singing a lonely song to her lost children."[21]

The lost children may refer to Native Americans kidnapped and brought to England. In that tale, Moshup is seen chasing a big white bird; that bird was a sailing ship. Another version of the lost children is that when Noepe became too crowded, Moshup turned his hundreds of children into fish of the sea.

Another story has Moshup relaxing in his cave in the Gay Head cliffs. He is never seen, but we know he is there because on misty mornings or cloudy afternoons, the smoke from his pipe appears as fog, encircling the cliffs of Gay Head.

THE LEGENDS OF MOSHUP help define and explain the origins of the topography of Gay Head. Native Americans have stories, sagas and fables to describe the geological formation of their natural surroundings. The stories provide a background for the morality of the Wampanoag as well. The culture of the Wampanoag is captured by the varied morals and messages in the fables, giving structure and substance to the Wampanoag people.

Moshup serves a viable role in Wampanoag theology. And the spirits of the Native Americans are not far removed from the god-like imaginations passed on through the years. Whether it's spirits or ghosts, haunted happenings or legendary tales, the stories carry a sense of wonder, amazement and belief at something we cannot explain. Therein lies the wonder.

NATIVES SHARE THE LEGEND of Katama, a beautiful native maiden. Her father, Wintucket, matched her in marriage with "a grumpy, old straight-hair." Later, whilst paddling her canoe gathering grasses for her wedding mat, she met Mattakessett, the handsome young chief of the Great Plain, a neighboring tribe.

According to legend, "His heart was smitten as with the arrow of fate as he saw the fair vision [of Katama] pushing her canoe among the rushes, and there on the shores of the beautiful waters love came to both." Unfortunately, the lovers were from two warring tribes and could not consummate their love. In an effort to avoid the anguish of their antagonist tribes, the lovers swam far out into the ocean, following the light of the moon on the waters. "And thus came death to Katama and Mattakessett."[22]

NOT ALL WAMPANOAG TALES are about Moshup. The Wampanoag did not have a devil in their culture or religion. Satan arrived when the English introduced the devil to the Wampanoag culture. However, before the white man, the Wampanoag believed in a mischief-maker or god of humor. Cheepi is akin to Loki in Norse mythology, Hermes of the Greek gods and Mercury, the trickster of the Romans. Cheepi created amusing or exasperating experiences for the Wampanoag, sometimes to teach a lesson, sometimes just for fun.

The legends of Cheepi, the magical mysterious mischief-maker of Wampanoag fame, live on. From the Wampanoag perspective, Cheepi "was a very bad and mischievous deity." One night, Cheepi caused the Indians to ruin their corn field by running around it, searching for him. "The Indians rushing out of doors charged the field on all sides, but were repulsed at every point by a fearful shape that seemed to be everywhere at once."[23] Cheepi fooled the Wampanoag into destroying their crop in an effort to teach them a lesson: honor the gods but don't let the corn go unharvested.

NOW LEAP FORWARD TO the forays of English explorers in the early years of the seventeenth century. The following tale is not a legend; it is a documented historical event that occurred in 1611. Epenow, a Wampanoag native of Martha's Vineyard, or Noepe, was kidnapped and brought back to England by Captain Edward Harlow. There, he was exhibited as a savage from the New World.

Epenow was smart and clever. He learned English. He realized the English were greedy and intent on finding gold. Epenow convinced the head of the Plymouth colony, Captain Ferdinando Gorges, that he knew there was gold on the Vineyard. Perhaps he deceived Gorges. Perhaps he knew there was iron pyrite or fool's gold at Gay Head. In any case, Epenow wanted to return home and, gauging the white man's weakness for gold, undertook deceit to return to the Vineyard. A ship under a Captain Hobson set off in search of gold. When the vessel reached the Vineyard, natives boarded it. Epenow engineered his escape by diving off the ship, under a hail of arrows. The English were nonplussed. They lost their captive as well as their dreams of gold.

THE SKELETON OF A large Indian, over six and a half feet, was uncovered on Hines Point, once known as Cedar Neck. It was noted that the native allegedly had a double set of teeth, both upper and lower, which certainly proved an unusual sight. A number of Native American implements were found in the area between Chunk's Hill (Oklahoma) and Cedar Neck (Hines Point), nearby where the Native Americans once lived.

THE LEGEND OF THE Indian brave Tashmoo explains the origin of the site known today as Lake Tashmoo. Quampeechee was a Native American woman who could predict events, a psychic or seer. Quampeechee could predict the location and means to discover the sweet waters that her son, Tashmoo, would find. Tashmoo proved to be Lake Tashmoo, adjacent to the Tisbury Water Works, which houses a brick building worth visiting. For more than a century, the waterworks provided water to Vineyard Haven.

ANOTHER WAMPANOAG MYTH EXPLAINS the rugged hillside of Peaked Hill, in Chilmark. "This part of the hilltop—Peaked Hill—is a wilderness of tumbled stones, and looks as though old Moshop might have dusted them out of his salt-shaker some time when the earth needed a great deal of seasoning."[24]

Two lovers sought solace from Moshup. They wanted to marry but sought to learn what Moshup would tell them about matrimony. "It was appointed that the two lovers should meet the Giant on Sampson's Hill, Chappaquiddick, and there they came."

Moshup took out his pipe and began to smoke. Now you must know that the pipe was in accord with the size of the man and that it took many bales of tobacco to fill it, so that when he was through and proceeded to knock the ashes out into the sea there arose a tremendous hissing sound and great clouds of smoke and vapor that filled the whole region with a dense fog.

When the fog lifted, there was a beautiful little island. "Thus was Nantucket born to meet the wants of a pair of Vineyard lovers."[25] Author Charles Hine continued, "So in Nantucket we have the authentic proof that the great Moshop once lived, and while it may gall our little neighbor to know that it was never intended in the original order of things and was merely created to fill a sudden emergency, it yet seems best to give the facts without bias."

"The time came when Moshop felt he was being crowded out, and there would soon be no room for such great fellows as himself." He gathered his children together. "By this time he had an infinite number of sons and daughters." Many years had passed, and Moshup and Squant were getting old. "Then Moshop called and told them to act as though they were bent on killing whales, whereupon they were all turned into killers (a fish so called). For you must know our giant was a magician as well as the fountain of all wisdom."[26]

Moshup and Squant retired past the Peaked Rocks and Black Rock to Zacks Cliffs, and as Charles Hine wrote, "Here they sought repose in a beach hummock and have never been seen more, though it is said the smoke of their camp fire is sometimes seen by those gifted with acute vision, and now and then 'Ol' Squant' is said to appear to certain merry gentlemen returning late at night from a visit to the sick, or otherwise."

Where the Old South Road entered Gay Head, it was there that, "the highway passes over Black Brook, a haunt of witches and goblins, where ghosts have been seen even of late years. The swampy, overgrown nature of the ground affords ample opportunity for hiding places, and there seems no good reason why ghosts should not abide here."[27]

ONE RATHER UNUSUAL CONTENTION by our early twentieth-century historian Charles Hine was that some of the first people who explored Martha's Vineyard were under the distinct impression that the island was home to a volcano and the extinct crater was located in the Devil's Den on the Gay Head Cliffs. Curiosity seekers have found charcoal, vitrified surfaces of stones, small stones "cemented together by melted sand" and many places with cinders. Legends and myths were passed on through the generations about the mystery of the volcanic origins of the Cliffs, which is where Moshup hides out even today.

Most likely the volcanic fables were an attempt to justify the variegated clay cliffs, the unusual eroding shoreline and the unique features peculiar to Gay Head. Tales of a volcanic eruption are every bit as justifiable to the untrained eye as the scientific explanations of great glacial upheavals.

IN 1711, THE LAND of Gay Head was set aside specifically for the Wampanoag tribe. However, it was not until 1870 that the town separated from Chilmark. The intent was to provide for Native Americans who had been granted the right to vote in exchange for surrendering their communally owned lands. To vote, one had to be a landowner. Since African American men had been granted enfranchisement with the Fifteenth Amendment, in 1870, Vineyarders felt obligated to offer the same to the Wampanoag male population.

And so it was that Gay Head came into existence. In 1998, the name of the town was changed to Aquinnah, an appellation more appropriate for the primarily Native American population. Aquinnah means "land under the hill."

RUMOR HAS IT THAT the Aquinnah Cultural Center is haunted. The house on the edge of the Cliffs, just below the viewing station and shops, was built by Edwin Vanderhoop in the 1890s. He was the first Wampanoag representative to the Massachusetts legislature, serving a term in 1888.

## CHILD DROWNS

### Small Girl Meets Death in Cistern

Elizabeth E. Vanderhoop, four year old daughter of Mr. and Mrs. Leonard F. Vanderhoop of Gay Head, was drowned in a cistern at the home of her parents Saturday forenoon. The child was playing about the premises and it is believed that she stepped on the iron manhole cover of the cistern which was broken in such a way as to tilt, and which dropped the little girl into about four feet of water.

According to the story told Boatswain William Nickerson of the coast guard station, who with some of his men responded to a call for aid, there was no one but the child's mother and a neighbor about the place. The splash of the child in the cistern first attracted attention and Mrs. Vanderhoop dropped a rope into the cistern which was grasped by the child. The child was apparently dazed, having probably struck the side of the cistern in the fall, and could do little to help herself. She rapidly became exhausted and sank.

The coastguardsmen succeeded in drawing the child from the water and tried to revive her, working until the arrival of Doctors T. C. Cosgrove and O. S. Mayhew, who pronounced her dead.

*Above*: Edwin Vanderhoop built his house overlooking the Gay Head shoreline in the 1890s. Today it serves as the Aquinnah Cultural Center, a rich source of Wampanoag lore and more, open to the public. *Photo by Joyce Dresser.*

*Left*: When the *Vineyard Gazette* published this story on December 21, 1928, no one foresaw haunted happenings nearly a century later. *Courtesy of Hilary Wallcox and the* Vineyard Gazette.

The house is considered haunted by some. And the haunting relates to an event that occurred some years after Vanderhoop built the house, late in the 1920s.

A true story lies behind this vision. Four-year-old Elizabeth Vanderhoop fell into a cistern and drowned back in 1928. Apparently, the little girl returns as an apparition or spirit; she is not ready, willing or able to move on. The image of the little girl is there, and several people have seen her. The story lingers. The presence is still affixed to the site.

We met with Amy Coffey upstairs at the Dr. Fisher House to hear her tale. Amy spent four summers living at the Vanderhoop Homestead in Aquinnah, "you know, the haunted house." Her friends said it was haunted and asked if she really wanted to stay there for the summer. She asserted, "I feel I am sensitive to things, and that dogs are sensitive to outside forces. And I have respect for the spirits around us."

The Vanderhoop Homestead was open from spring to fall, as its water is linked to the shops at the Cliffs, which are closed off-season. The house dates to the 1890s; it was the ancestral home of the Vanderhoops, with Vanderhoop portraits, pictures and books on the walls and shelves of the building.

"As long as you're respectful of the property and don't change things, you'll be fine. That was how to live there," said Amy, "to respect the property and not change it."

She continued, "I felt I had a conversation with a force, with an energy, that was there. And those people who had less respect for the spirits were haunted more than me."

Amy felt it was important to show respect to the spirits who live there: "I did stay there one Halloween night, alone. And then I felt it was the right thing to leave. I felt comfortable on Halloween, but not any longer than that."

Amy heard, definitely heard, footsteps on the stairs. There were guests in the house, but they were not making those footsteps. And she felt a hug, a real comfortable hug. "It was definitely the little girl. I felt it. It was in the hallway. And it was because I tried to help them. The little girl presented herself to me a couple of times, but I'm not sure if I wanted to see her, or actually did see her."

One time, Amy's sister came to visit. She said she felt the mother's grief over the death of her little girl. It was a very real and powerful sensation.

The grass never grows around the cistern where the little girl drowned. And there's a portrait of the little girl and her mother. In the image, the girl's hand is twisted.

A roommate had a dog at the Vanderhoop Homestead one summer. The dog got sick and eventually died. The next summer, on her first night at the Homestead, Amy felt that dog jump on her bed and curl up, right next to her. She said it felt like a spiritual connection with the dog.

The fellow whose dog died has seen an apparition of the little girl in the mirror a couple of times. More than once he commented, "The little girl was unhappy last night."

~

WE FOUND ANOTHER SUMMER tenant of the Vanderhoop Homestead and met with Karen Coffey of Vineyard Haven.

One summer, Karen (no relation to Amy) lived at the Vanderhoop Homestead with three roommates: a baker, a female summer cop and a restaurant worker. Karen was a housecleaner.

At 2:00 a.m., all the doors were locked. In the morning, the doors were unlocked. One night, all the items on Karen's bureau were brushed onto the floor. The dog and the cat each fell down the stairs.

The summer cop saw a little girl outside when she came home and thought it was Karen; however, Karen was sound asleep in bed. The piano would play by itself.

One night, Karen heard footsteps pacing in the hall. The steps stopped outside Karen's door. She sat up, couldn't breathe and said aloud, "This isn't happening." The footsteps receded.

Years before, Nanetta Vanderhoop fell down stairs in the house and was paralyzed. And the tale of Elizabeth Vanderhoop, the little girl who drowned in the well, occurred here.

Karen suggested that "some people are not sensitive to ghosts. Ghosts leave an imprint of where they lived." The Vanderhoop Homestead, now the Aquinnah Cultural Center, certainly seems to bear its share of spectral experiences.

And a rumor posits that a previous structure on this site was a station on the Underground Railroad.

# 6

# CHILMARK ORDINARIES

We read the words of historian Charles Banks on the requirement in colonial days that innkeepers provide entertainment and libations to travelers. Innkeepers were forbidden, however, to sell alcohol to Indians; if they did, a stiff fine would be levied.

Some towns, like Chilmark, were so small it was inconvenient to have to have an inn; in such cases, locals were allowed to serve alcohol to "transient guests" in private homes. A room would be set aside where guests could, "smoke, drink and play cards and hear the village gossip from the convivial patrons of this portion of the ordinary."[28]

Because private homes substituted for inns or ordinaries in small communities such as Chilmark, we cannot track down ghosts or spirits unless the homeowner recorded any such event. A couple of private homes do convey a sense of the poltergeist, although both are tangential to actual ghost sightings.

In the 1990s, a couple purchased the old Mayhew-Copley house, aka the Luce homestead, on South Road, built in 1722. Elsie Fenner ran Wayside Farm in the 1950s. According to Holly Nadler in *Haunted Island*, Fenner was "a farm lady, innkeeper, and real estate agent, she also wrote the Chilmark town column for the *Vineyard Gazette*." Turns out Fenner may still be typing away, as the homeowners often heard the sound of typing coming from the second floor.

More than one guest at Wayside Farm encountered the spectral typist. "She wears an old fashioned dark dress, with a similarly old fashioned line of buttons down the back. She stands in the central juncture of the bedroom, motionless, like a child banished to the corner."[29]

We checked with the *Vineyard Gazette* to see if Elsie Fenner was indeed still filing the Chilmark column. No, indeed, Elsie Fenner passed away in 1967. Hilary Wallcox, *Gazette* librarian, responded to our inquiry: "Regarding Elsie Fenner, the Gazette did not start to list bylines for the Chilmark Column until 1965, so it's hard to know for certain who was writing the column in the 30s, 40s, and 50s."

We checked with Elsie Fenner's nephew, Frank. He remembered his aunt Elsie quite well. "She was quite a character," he recalled. "I came home from Vietnam in '67, and they say she stayed alive just to see me."

Frank Fenner mentioned that his aunt was a nurse during World War I. She served as chief nurse at Camp Lee, Virginia. During the Second World War, Elsie Fenner organized surgical dressing units for the Red Cross in various towns to aid wounded soldiers.

Nothing in Elsie Fenner's life indicates she had a reason to haunt her old house, and Frank had no recollection of spectral experiences. However, once a character, always a character. Perhaps Elsie just wanted to keep on typing through the years.

~

THE DAUGHTER OF A friend caught sight of a ghostly apparition in an old Chilmark house, but the spirit vanished into thin air. After seeing an unknown woman standing in the window of a pre–Revolutionary War house in Chilmark (since demolished), the daughter now claims what she initially witnessed was most likely a piece of plastic covering a broken window waving in the breeze. Such are the probable explanations of some ghost stories.

~

PATTY EGAN SHARED A story of a house in Chilmark, located on North Road. "I believe part of it, or all of it, was moved from Tea Lane. It used to be part of the Cagney estate." A fellow who grew up there has memories of that house, tales of a stereo being turned on in the morning to classical music, a spectral image of someone or something looking down from upstairs. There are numerous stories of that house. "It is haunted," she said. "You know, I can feel it."

ANOTHER CHILMARK HOUSE BEARS scrutiny. Although this eighteenth-century structure has since been torn down, it had an intriguing history, as well as a more recent past. The house was built in 1735 and served as headquarters for the British when they marched up island on the Vineyard in September 1778. The story goes that when the redcoats accosted the owners, searching for weapons or gunpowder, one daughter sat on a barrel near the fireplace while the British searched the house. The barrel was filled with gunpowder but never discovered.

In more recent years, a tenant who rented the house reported his radio turned on and off on its own. With new tenants, it took a while to feel comfortable with unusual actions. The owners, Catie and Erik Blake, felt the house was haunted. They often heard footsteps upstairs that could not be accounted for. The antique clock in the kitchen had no batteries yet continued to tick. An electric blender would turn on or off, yet was not plugged in. Strange sounds erupted at unusual times. Dogs would growl, looking up at the attic.

One time the homeowners heard a hissing sound, suspiciously haunting. Upon investigation, it turned out a pipe had burst in the hot water heater and water was spewing out all over the basement. That's when the homeowners determined it was time to tear down the house and rebuild.

ONE VINEYARD SITE RETAINS its aura of mystery through generations. Charles Hine set the tone in his 1908 tome: "Summer estate known as 'Windygates', which covers the bluffs of Wesquabsque or Chilmark Cliffs, from which can be had a magnificent survey of the ocean."[30] The mysteries and majesty of Windy Gates continue to mesmerize Vineyarders.

An early twentieth-century description of Windy Gates couches a laudatory commentary in a long letter to the *Gazette* dated 1905, written by Chilmark neighbor Haig Adadourian. "The lovely home referred to is situated in the midst of a charming sylvan scenery, which in attractiveness cannot be surpassed by any spot on the Island."

Lucy Sanford purchased the property in 1891 and invested heavily in renovations. Windy Gates comprised some three hundred acres with three miles of macadamized roads, walks and paths. Landscaping included a rose-

Lucy Stafford, a Gilded Age widow, transformed her Windy Gates mansion into a veritable eccentric estate. Some have seen her or members of her entourage still on site. *Courtesy of the Martha's Vineyard Museum.*

draped pergola, terraces, a bridged Mill Brook, a tennis court and a windmill to pump water into a reservoir. "The house contains nearly all the modern conveniences of a city residence."

Three-quarters of a century later, *Gazette* editorialist Joseph Chase Allen reported that since the Revolution, nothing had upset the island as much as the construction of Windy Gates, "chiefly by the way that money was being spent to the utter disregard of the proprietors who spent it."

Lucy Sanford paid to have the farmhouse enlarged and elegantly appointed. The bathroom included Italian tile wainscoting and gold-plated fixtures. The work on the house was "the most elaborate that the Island had ever seen." Stables were built and carriages purchased, but no horses arrived; the pigsty was illuminated so the sow could see in the dark. Reporter Allen observed, "Yet while she lived and was able to gratify her aims and ambitions, she came as near to turning the Island upside-down as anyone had ever done up to that time."

Of the eccentric history of the estate, another *Gazette* reporter, Rebecca Orr, wrote, "Mrs. Sanford kept changing her mind about what she wanted so just as much seemed to be torn down each day as constructed."[31]

Daughter Mary Kobbe and handyman-bicycle salesman Jack Seals (jack of all trades) lived with Mrs. Sanford during renovations. Once the house was completed, Mary married a mysterious count. The newlyweds, Jack Seals and Lucy Sanford, cohabited in luxurious style, emulating Newport's Gilded Age by hosting elegant parties and making a name for themselves with their festivities. The quartet participated in an elegant, fanciful lifestyle, quite unlike their rural Chilmark neighbors.

The count enticed Mrs. Sanford to invest in South American railroad stocks, then disappeared. Both Mary Kobbe and Jack Seals died under mysterious circumstances. Lucy Sanford kept their ashes in urns on the mantel. The railroad stocks lost their value.

Lucy Sanford apparently lost everything, and with her daughter dead, the count disappeared; she lost her mind as well as her money. (Later, it turned out that the railway stocks had appreciated in value to more than a $100,000.)

~

OVER THE YEARS, WINDY GATES has undergone renovations and repairs, as well as changes in ownership. The estate continues to draw interest, with "occasional requests for a showing of the bathroom in which Mrs. Lucy Sanford, who put the place on the map in the 19th century, was said to have installed golden fixtures."[32]

People hired as caretakers to monitor the property and live in the carriage house on site have experienced unusual sights and sounds they cannot explain. Over the years, the strange feeling people get while they are at Windy Gates, the unexplained sounds, the claims of apparitions of a man dressed in clothing from another century, have remained constant. As author Max Hart admonished, "It is a place to be avoided on Halloween."[33]

Windy Gates gives rise to legends from years gone by. "The old manor nestled in the dark woods just feet from the Wequobsket cliffs is perhaps the

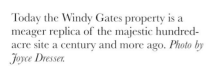

Today the Windy Gates property is a meager replica of the majestic hundred-acre site a century and more ago. *Photo by Joyce Dresser.*

most notoriously haunted house on Martha's Vineyard." A female figure glimpsed in the gloaming is the ghost of a woman whose husband perished on a whaleship lost at sea. In her anguish and grief, she was said to have jumped off Wequobsket cliffs to her death. Some say a male apparition still frequents the grounds, reliving a life of luxury tarnished by disaster.

A young couple picnicked on site one day. They were startled to see a man appear nearby and watch them. As the woman described the visitor, "He looked like someone from Masterpiece Theatre, you know in a long black jacket and a sort of brocaded vest." And he just disappeared.

Another spectral sighting was described: "A lady in white has shown up here and there, either traipsing through the woods or floating over the fields, her feet raised several inches from the ground."[34]

Roger Baldwin, founder of the ACLU, bought and lived at Windy Gates as his summer home. Later, one tenant noted, "Our own inexplicable sighting of heavenly lights and a woman in white dancing came late one night and was later explained to us as the birthday appearance of Baldwin's daughter Helen, who had died years earlier."[35]

An update of Windy Gates by Rachel Orr noted that the Land Bank turned down acquisition of 1,000 feet of shoreline consisting of 105 acres from South Road to the ocean. The 100-foot-high cliff and extensive wetlands required too much work to be successfully managed by the Land Bank.

# 7

# COTTAGE CITY

Next, we check in on Oak Bluffs, for many years listed as the northwestern segment of the town of Edgartown. This sylvan site spawned the Methodist campground and later the Oak Bluffs Land & Wharf Company, which developed the first planned summer residential community in the country. In the last quarter of the nineteenth century, people of this section of Edgartown grew outraged by the failure of the town fathers to provide a bridge over the lagoon or put any money into local town services. A movement arose to secede from Edgartown.

By 1880, a measure to secede passed the Massachusetts state legislature, and the town of Cottage City was born. The Methodist campground, Wesleyan Grove, was then bursting with five hundred summer cottages. Cottage City thrived with the growth of the Oak Bluffs Land & Wharf Company. The amusement park atmosphere in the downtown village, spurred by the burgeoning steamship service, multiple majestic hotels, and an expansive electric trolley system completed the picture. The reputation of this fabled vacation community attracted growing crowds and an ever-expanding aura of success. The new town was assured prominence even as its progenitor, Edgartown, suffered loss of income due to the dearth of the whaling industry.

WE RECALL THE LEGEND of the three liberty pole girls—Polly Daggett, Parnell Manter and Marie Allen—from the days of the Revolutionary War. The British ship *Unicorn* entered Vineyard Haven Harbor with a broken spar in the spring of 1778. The captain informed the townspeople that he would take the local liberty pole for his broken spar. The three young women had other plans. That night, they used an auger to drill holes in the famed pole. They poured in gunpowder and set a fuse to their explosive. Within moments, the liberty pole lay shattered on the ground. We have located the gravestones of these three women, and we have a tale or two to share about their lives after the liberty pole incident.

Many anecdotes celebrate the early days of Oak Bluffs. An Eastville inn in the vicinity of the Martha's Vineyard Hospital was a place of frivolity in the late seventeenth century. It is said that one, and perhaps two, of the liberty pole ladies worked at Claghorn's, as the ordinary was called.

Polly Hillman, née Daggett, was psychic and predicted matters relating to her family. Whether this tale is true or not, it lingers as an element of Vineyard history.

Known as Aunt Hillman, Polly was "a woman of strong character and great ability; she left a lasting impression on those who came in contact with her."[36] Hillman had a gift of prophecy or second sight that was nearly incomprehensibly accurate.

When Captain William Daggett failed to return home as scheduled, Polly went to see his wife; in a sanguine manner, she told his wife to prepare dinner, as he was on his way. Soon, his ship was spotted rounding West Chop, heading home in time for dinner.

Another, more unfortunate, incident occurred that involved her brother Silas Daggett. "Aunt Hillman saw her brother Silas Daggett lying on the shore with a bruise on his forehead." That she "saw" him indicates that Aunt Hillman was a seer, a psychic. "He was later found drowned and washed up with a bruised head, as she had foretold."[37]

Another liberty pole lady, Parnell Manter, fell in love with a local man, but her father forbade her to see him. She pined away over the separation.

The ambitious suitor clambered up a cherry tree in her backyard, adjacent to her bedroom window. Parnell saw her lover, but "the girl caught a cold which resulted in her death. During her sickness she had a trance in which she visited Heaven and it was there revealed to her that she must die." She was but twenty years old when she died.

MOONCUSSERS REIGNED SUPREME OFF the Barbary Coast, as Eastville was known back in the day. A mooncusser is a pirate. On a typically dark and moonless night, the mooncusser hung a lantern on the shore, hoping to distract a captain to run his ship to the light. When the ship was close to shore, or run aground, the mooncusser boarded the wrecked vessel and stole what he could. While the story sounds mythical, there definitely were some seedy characters who performed unsavory activities among those who frequented the shores of Eastville.

IN THE 1890S, OAK Bluffs was in the throes of a rash of arson. The Sea View House burned in 1892. The Highland House burned. The owner of the Wesley Hotel was arrested on site trying to torch his hotel for insurance monies and served time in jail. And the Corbin Norton House, on the edge of Ocean Park, was set afire.

The Corbin-Norton House today, after a complete rebuild following the 2001 fire. And was it spectral arson, or electrical malfunction? *Photo by Joyce Dresser.*

"When tech gazillionaire Peter Norton's gorgeous Queen Anne burned down in 2001, there were those who didn't believe that faulty wiring was to blame. According to local ghost hunter Holly Nadler, sisters Julie and Loulou Danzell, the Oak Bluffs arsonists of 1894, seemed like more likely spirited suspects."[38]

The two Danzell sisters worked as maids in the Corbin Norton house on Ocean Park. "Skeptics will say it's only a coincidence that the home of the pyromaniacs burst into flames more than a hundred years after the young firebugs had been dragged off in chains."[39]

Peter Norton rebuilt his house in 2002, just as Philip Corbin had done after his house was torched after the 1894 fire. The house is as impressive and outstanding as ever.

~

IN A MORE CURRENT era, still in Oak Bluffs, we appreciate the following tale, which relates a simple dinner at a prominent Circuit Avenue restaurant.

"I never knew my grandmother, my mother's mother," wrote Joan B. "She died before my parents were married and I was born, but I've always felt a closeness to her through stories my mom would tell me about her, and also the essence of her I feel when I'm on the Vineyard. She is buried on the Vineyard and I visit her every time I'm there."

Joan spent summers on the Vineyard as a child, and as an adult, she is obsessed with the charm and beauty of the Island.

She continued, "Chances are she might have visited me a few years ago!!!" Joan added an excerpt from a post she wrote:

> On the very haunted island of Martha's Vineyard, in the town of Oak Bluffs, in a restored Victorian home was a restaurant called The Sweet Life Café. In this house in the 1930s lived a daughter and her mother. In this house, the mother passed away. That woman was my grandmother and the daughter was my mother.

Now the story gets interesting:

> A few years ago my daughter Deb and I decided to treat ourselves to dinner at the Sweet Life Café. We'd never eaten there but felt the time was right. It was around 5 o'clock on a beautiful cloudless and breezeless May evening

*so we opted to sit on the patio in the garden as it was empty and peaceful. The tables were beautifully laid out and each had on it a small hurricane lamp with a candle in it.*

We're getting there.

*We looked around and noticed that the candles on all the tables but ours were lit! Our waitress re-lit ours. The candle went out. Again she lit it. Again it went out. She came back with a new candle. Again, out it went. Again she re-lit it to no avail. My daughter and I joked that our grandmothers were joining us and were definitely in a playful mood.*

And now the denouement:

*Later that evening as my daughter and I were passing by the restaurant we looked in at the patio.... The candle on the table we had been sitting at was burning brightly!*

WHILE JOAN B.'S GRANDMOTHER was playful, Susan W. experienced another event that proved hauntingly impressive and much more surreal.

To summarize Susan's drama, we travel back a few decades when she was a college student, assigned to open the family's campground cottage for the season. The family had purchased the house some years before from a woman who left the Vineyard for Florida; the elderly woman passed away shortly before Susan assumed her role of opening up the cottage.

Susan brought a girlfriend down for the weekend. They had twin beds in the second-story bedroom of the Clinton Avenue house. All was well until they went to bed. In the middle of the night, Susan awoke. She felt a presence moving surreptitiously right by her bed. She called out to her girlfriend to go back to bed. The girlfriend was fast asleep. Susan felt the image pass her, brushing against the bed, and open the door to go up the stairs to the attic. Too frightened to follow, Susan did her best to roll over and go back to sleep, hoping, praying it was a bad dream. In the morning, she confided in her girlfriend, who had heard and seen nothing.

Susan had a couple more strange encounters to report. Her sister's boyfriend approached the house one day and knocked on the door. When

Campground cottages were built in Westleyan Grove from 1857 to 1877. Designed as summer respites, many a house has a haunted history. *Photo by Joyce Dresser.*

the sister immediately opened the door, the boyfriend was taken aback. He had just seen a woman in the upstairs window. The sister said she was alone in the house.

Another time, Susan was on the couch, downstairs, with her boyfriend. He felt a presence in the house and urged Susan to leave right away. The house is no longer in Susan's family. Who knows who lives there now?!

While these incidents happened many decades ago, it is of interest that Susan Wilson has absolute recall of the experience, how she reacted then and how she feels about it today. Following are her responses to our inquiry in January 2020:

*Are you frightened when you recall the experience?* "Not at all. After the initial episode, we more or less took the manifestations (if that's what they were) as a kind of an inside joke."

*When your family sold the house, did they disclose the unnamed guest who apparently came with the house?* "By the time they decided to sell, the manifestations had stopped (which lent the whole thing some believability.) We told ourselves that the ghost was pleased to get the teenagers out of the house."

*Do you have anything else to add?* "It was a weird experience but we were adolescents and extremely susceptible to the power of suggestion."

So, there you have it. It would seem that the ghost of the previous owner, an elderly woman who moved to Florida, returned and remained in the house in a spectral status. By the time the family was ready to sell the property, the ghost was ready to move on.

~

ROBYN WINGATE SHARES A tale from her youth that frightened her: "Across from the milk company on School Street were some vacant houses. My brother and I went in there one time and saw a life-like image that scared us. I can see the outline in my mind today. It was a guy, maybe in his thirties. I was about eight years old. We never went back there."

~

IN THE SUMMER OF 2018 Mary Elizabeth Surprenant worked at the Book Den East in Oak Bluffs. When she was there by herself, she said, "I felt a tapping, a knocking sound. It was interesting but not frightening." She added, "I can only admit to hearing tapping and creaking and possible footsteps when I was alone there." That makes it worthwhile to stop in and check out the bookstore.

~

## THE GREAT AND GENERAL COURT WILL BE IN SECESSION?

This story isn't the least bit scary, unless you take it to the extreme. And we include this tale not for its haunting drama but because it parallels the real-life drama that occurred a century prior, in 1880. The village that sprouted around Lake Anthony was an amalgam of Wesleyan Grove Methodist Camp-Meeting Association and the Oak Bluffs Land & Wharf Company. Residents of these two combined communities resented that the town fathers of Edgartown refused to use tax money to improve the local area. Hence, a movement was launched to secede from Edgartown.

This was accomplished in 1880 with the formation of the town known as Cottage City. Twenty-seven years later, in 1907, the name was changed to Oak Bluffs, but the secession had succeeded.

Now leap forward seventy years to the quiet, peaceful chill of the winter of 1977. The Great and General Court of the Commonwealth of Massachusetts (which dates to 1629) took it upon itself to redistrict county representation for the Cape and islands. The result was that Martha's Vineyard lost its representative in the state legislature. In response, perhaps at a local cocktail party, perhaps an Art Buchwald what-if parody, an idea was promulgated that the Vineyard should secede from Massachusetts.

Vineyarders seriously considered withdrawing from Massachusetts and signing on with other states that indicated an interest in absorbing them, such as Connecticut, New Hampshire, Nevada and Vermont. And if that didn't succeed, rascally islanders considered establishing identity as a new state, independent altogether even from the United States.

As Mike Seccombe wrote, an aide to the governor of Maine was quoted in the papers as saying that state had split in 1820 from Massachusetts out of "a feeling of remoteness" and pointedly noted Maine had one representative for every two thousand people.

Everett Poole, a Chilmark selectman, recalled, "The governor of Vermont sent me a letter with half a gallon of maple syrup and said his state would love to have a sea coast. I sent him back four pints of quahaug chowder."

John Alley, one of the secession ringleaders from West Tisbury, was also courted by Governor Snelling:

> He rang me, when I was running the general store one day. I just thought it was a crank call and I said, "Yeah, sure," and I hung up. And the guy rang back and said, "No, I really am the governor of Vermont." Later he came in the store two or three times. I got letters from him saying he would be glad to have Vermont annex Martha's Vineyard.

Nothing came of the effort, although it did spark a bit of publicity and gave people something to talk about over the long, cold, lonely weeks of winter. The decision by the General Court remained in effect, but Vineyarders did gain a bit of empathy from the statehouse over the challenges of island life.[40]

# 8

# HOLMES HOLE

We now visit the little village of Vineyard Haven, formerly Holmes Hole, host of the protective harbor and center of commercial traffic on the Vineyard. For three centuries, the village was part of what is now West Tisbury, but the towns diverged economically in 1892. West Tisbury retained its agrarian focus, and Tisbury aligned itself with the harbor.

～

GHOSTS, YOU ASK? TRY a couple of patients from the old Marine hospital. Spirits, you wonder? Listen to ghost stories told in the days of the St. Pierre Camp.

The building that houses the Martha's Vineyard Museum was built in 1895 as the Marine Hospital. It closed in 1952. The St. Pierre School of Sport ran a children's summer camp on site from 1959 to 2007. In 2011, the museum purchased the property, renovated it and moved in in 2019.

Shortly after it opened, the Marine Hospital met the needs of sailors injured in the Portland Gale of November 1898. Dozens of ships sank in the harbor, and many crew members were injured. Residents of the Marine Hospital were sailors, injured or ill from life at sea. Many residents became characters in the community. The Marine Cemetery off Canterbury Lane is a final resting place for victims of nautical disasters.

Captain Corey Hamilton (1868–1945) was from Nova Scotia. He was incapacitated by an injury that caused him to be severely stooped over. It was

The building that houses the Martha's Vineyard Museum in Vineyard Haven is a rich source of island artifacts as well as a repository of numerous spectral stories. *Photo by Joyce Dresser.*

only with two short canes that he managed to get around. For years, he was a resident of the hospital. He would hobble down to the little scallop shack by the lagoon, where he built impressive model ships. His artistic scenes included wharves, houses and trees.

Hamilton had an argument with the Marine Hospital and moved out, taking up residence in a little boat nearby, ashore in the winter and afloat in season. It was a sight to see him motor around the harbor, his head just poking over the deck.

Captain Anton Svenson (1888–1951), a Swede, was admitted in 1922 and lived at the hospital until his death. He was a grumpy old man, unless you got to know him. He, too, made ship models in the scallop shack, succeeding Hamilton as the artist in residence.

Captain John Ivory sailed on clipper ships in his youth and lived for a time in the Far East. Ivory was often drunk but continued his predecessors' tradition of artistic endeavors. With little income due to other expenses, Ivory painted on cardboard, linoleum and canvas; he made brushes from hair and painted with used house paint.

Ivory lived in the boat Corey Hamilton had called home. His painting *Governor Robie* is in the Vineyard Haven Library. Jane Slater knew Ivory.

David Noble worked on an oil tanker and suffered a creeping paralysis. He was admitted to the Marine Hospital in 1933. In 1949, he took up ham radio operation and spoke with operators all over the world on his transmitter. His wall was covered with cards from contacts. Niece Kathy Noble Case and family moved to the island and cared for him. He died in 1968.

~

BOW VAN RIPER, THE librarian of the Martha's Vineyard Museum, confirmed, "I've heard a lot of St. Pierre Camp alums say that the Marine Hospital felt spooky." He went on: "I've never heard anyone describe an actual apparition or other encounter with a ghost."

Two of David Perzanowski's children attended the St. Pierre School of Sport. Elena recalled,

> I never had any legit ghost stories where I myself saw or experienced one, but as a nervous child with an overactive imagination, there was one occurrence that stood out to me that still makes my stomach sink. One day we were playing four square before pickup time. The ball fell out of play and bounced towards an open window/vent to the basement. One of the counselors tells us, "If that goes into the basement, you have to go down there with all the spirits and get it."

Elena continued. "I was afraid that either Steven or I would lose the ball and have to go down there. I probably stopped playing four square altogether. But yes, the older kids always told us it was haunted and it felt like the counselors would only allude to the hauntings whenever we acted up."

She added, "I like to imagine the training manual said 'DON'T TELL CAMPERS ABOUT THE GHOSTS THAT INHABIT THIS PLACE… unless they're being little brats.'"

Her brother Steven remembered, "Going down the stairs into a hallway, an orb was seen at the other end of the hall. It went down another set of stairs, disappeared. The stairs led to a door in the cellar….We were afraid to go in."

David Perzanowski summed up the memories. "In general the kids would sneak around the building and try to look into the cellar. It was scary… gurneys and beds down there…but nothing really happened." The warning was stark: "One of the main things….STAY OUT OF THE CELLAR!"

While school committees and town meetings haggle over repairs or replacement of the ancient Tisbury School (circa 1929), Scotty still makes his presence known now and then. *Photo by Joyce Dresser.*

IN THE MID-1800s, THE Tisbury school system consisted of seven districts located in various parts of Holmes Hole and what is now West Tisbury, as the two towns were one until 1892. Students would walk to their local school; school buses didn't emerge until the early twentieth century. The first centrally located school in Tisbury was built on Center Street, near the town tennis courts, in 1854. By the 1920s, that school was ready to be replaced.

An off-island company was hired to build a new school under the direction of Thane Cottrell. Thane's younger brother Herbert was part of the crew. Herb was twenty-one, half the age of his elder brother.

School construction began along West Spring Street, right where the school stands today. As Chris Baer reported,

> *Tragedy struck on the evening of Wednesday, July 17, 1929. The brothers were inspecting the crew's work, and as a family member recalled, a storm was coming, and the brothers needed to secure the site. While standing on a girder on the third floor of the framework, Herbert stepped backward and lost his balance. He fell through a square hole left for a stairwell or*

*chimney, and plummeted more than 50 feet into the basement. He died almost instantly.*[41]

Thane Cottrell and his company completed work on the Tisbury School, and students entered the new building on Spring Street. The first Tisbury High School class graduated in the spring of 1930; the school has been in operation ever since.

The spirit of Herbert Cottrell lives on. According to Baer, a number of Tisbury School students have encountered Scottie, as the ghost of young Cottrell is known. He haunts the old school, flicking the lights on and off. Former student Bonnie (Baptiste) Bassett wrote, "I remember this. When the Tisbury School was being constructed, a man fell and was then buried in cement. If you were around the school at midnight, you would see the ghost or hear him screaming!"

Richie Smith worked at the Tisbury School for years and had one strange experience. On a summer evening, Richie was on the third floor of the Tisbury School, painting his office. He got a tingly feeling. He was painting behind the open office door, and the door began to nudge him, more than once. It was a forceful push. Richie said, "Hey, I'm just trying to make your school nicer." Richie said it was spooky.

Glenn Maciel was a custodian at the school for many years, arriving at work early in the day. One time, he showed up between 4:00 and 5:00 a.m. with his dog, Max. The dog froze, whimpered and would not move down the hall. What made the dog stop? Glenn reportedly saw a spectral image at the end of the hallway. It was the image of one of the custodians named Scottie. Scottie was dead, yet people felt his presence. "When they put up the new addition, in 1995, no more Scottie. We wonder if he will return when they do the renovations of the Tisbury School," sayed Glenn's wife, who confirmed his sightings.

Reportedly, Scottie, the spectral intruder, spent years in Janet Stiller's classroom closet on the third floor.

We checked in with Kerry Alley, who worked for decades at the Tisbury School. "I heard the rumors," he said, "but it was before my time." Alley said that when he was a kid going to school in Oak Bluffs, there was a janitor at the Tisbury School named Scottie. Perhaps it is the ghost of Scottie who still pushes a broom up and down the hallways.

Kerry suggested we get in touch with Bobby Gale, head custodian of the school for many years. He served as head custodian and should know what was going on. Bobby Gale graduated from the Tisbury School in 1955. He'd

The 1720 House was built up-island and floated down Vineyard Sound around 1800. A house with that much history must have some unusual stories to share. *Photo by Joyce Dresser.*

heard about the employee who fell to his death back in 1929. "He landed in the boiler room," said Gale.

According to Bobby Gale, Scottie was a school custodian in the school during the 1940s and '50s. Bobby Gale worked as a custodian there as well. He recalled, "I've had a lot of fun with the kids. During parent-teacher night I'd take the kids down to see the ghost in the boiler room." That was all. He said he used to work nights and had "never seen or heard a ghost." So there you have it.

Or do you?

Could Scottie be a ghost of the old custodian or a ghost of the employee who died when the school was built back in 1929?

THE 1720 HOUSE WAS floated down Vineyard Sound on a raft from Cape Higgon on the Vineyard North Shore by John Cleveland, a master mariner originally from Nantucket. He had purchased the structure in the 1700s

This innocuous house on Spring Street, Vineyard Haven, backs up to another house where spirits are known to hang out. *Photo by Joyce Dresser.*

from the parents of Catherine Look, whom he married in 1775. The house was brought into Vineyard Haven Harbor, hauled off the raft and up the shore by oxen. Cleveland's neighbors were impressed.

The house was originally built in the northwest corner of West Tisbury in 1744. (Where the date 1720 came from is anyone's guess.) According to Jim Norton, the house was moved to Vineyard Haven prior to 1809.

An 1875 photo of the house shows a simple Cape; now it has a mansard roof. Over the years, the house was moved back from the roadway. A porch was added, as well as a kitchen ell; the porch was removed. The house was renamed Heart's Content in 1882. Charles Norton bought the house in 1903. Olympic contender Bayes Norton was born there (father of Jim).[42]

A former employee suggested that "something had to have happened here in this three-hundred-plus-year-old house." The bathroom by the dining room on the first floor has to be kept locked on the outside. "One day it went flying open. No way wind could have done that. It was physically locked on the outside."

A local paranormal feels the energy of the 1720 House whenever she drives by.

IN HER VINEYARD HAVEN apartment, Mary Giordano noticed that on occasion, the lights flickered. Sometimes it's the overhead light in the dining room; at other times it's one of two floor lamps, plugged into the same outlet in the living room. Strange. Mary tightened the bulbs, but it keeps happening. She has no logical explanation for lights that flicker from time to time.

Mary is not afraid but wonders if perhaps someone from her past or even the future is sending her a message, trying to make his/her presence known.

Early in the new year, Mary awoke at 4:30 a.m. to the strong odor of cigarette smoke. This has happened in the apartment before. Mary doesn't smoke. She's not aware of anyone else in the building who smokes, especially in the middle of the night.

It is a strange sensation, but again, Mary is not afraid.

How did I learn about Mary's poltergeist? I had a dental appointment to repair a chipped tooth, a tooth I chipped back in 1954 as an irascible second grader playing a game of hide-and-seek. I closed my eyes and spun around, my face landing against the brick wall of Jefferson Elementary School, chipping my tooth.

I picked up the chip, and the teacher in charge of recess managed to save it and give it to my parents. The dentist was unable to repair it, so I lived with a chipped front tooth for the next seventy or so years.

When I finished my saga, Mary asked what I was up to; I told her ghost stories was on my agenda. She shared her tale of flickering lights and the acrid smell of cigarette smoke.

One never knows whence a ghost story will emerge. Some people believe in the Baader-Meinhof Phenomenon that we don't recognize a pattern or a system or the frequency of a given item until it reaches our conscience in several specific occasions. That seems to be my story: I never got into ghost stories until this topic was put on my plate, and now ghostly tales erupt in every corner of my surroundings.

Karen Coffey spent thirty years cleaning houses across the island: sea captains' houses, farmers' houses. "Every house that I have been in has some presence," she said; her cleaning company was called Haunted House Cleaning Company. Karen Coffey is a well-known Vineyarder who considers herself a paranormal. She is someone who knows ghosts. "I can sense a ghost," she confirmed.

Paranormal Karen Coffey lived in the Luce House for thirty years. Her spectral experiences would fill a book. *Photo by Joyce Dresser.*

*Above*: The Village Cemetery in Vineyard Haven holds the grave of Katharine Cornell, as well as numerous other spirits still floating around. *Photo by Thomas Dresser.*

*Left*: Karen Coffey is experienced in finding ghosts. The ghost of Babe Duncan, a deceased woodworker, shelters in her Vineyard Haven shop Pyewacket's. *Photo by Joyce Dresser.*

"A ghost led an incomplete life," she said. "Their relationship with life has not been completed. It is like a black-and-white negative. A ghost leaves a piece of itself in the old house." The image of the person stays in the house; the ghost needs people to connect with them.

For many years, Karen lived in the Luce House on Centre Street in Vineyard Haven, almost back to back with the house where Mary Giordano experienced flickering lights and unusual sounds. The first night Karen spent in house, alone, at about two o'clock in the morning, she witnessed a tall lady appear at the foot of her bed. "She was very proud, with her chin raised," Karen recalled. "She asked me to take good care of the house."

Coffey described the background of the Jonathan Luce House. It was built in the early nineteenth century in what is considered the historic district of Vineyard Haven. Many prominent sea captains hired architect James D. Peakes to build their houses. Peakes later became an undertaker and town postmaster (1861 to 1881).

Jonathan Luce (1792–1872) was a mariner and served as deputy sheriff in Holmes Hole. In 1811, Luce married Clara Cooke; they had one son, William Cook Luce, who was murdered in his dry goods shop on Union Street in 1863.

Luce married his second wife, Sarah Holmes Dunham, in 1816. The couple had eight children. She is buried in the Village Cemetery on Franklin Street. The Luces' granddaughter married the son of James Peakes. Tragically, the young couple died in a maritime disaster. Jonathan Luce suffered a good deal of tragedy in his life. Peakes was still close to Jonathan Luce and served as executor to the Luce estate.

Ghosts are confused. More often than not they encountered tragedy when they were alive; a ghost experienced an incomplete relationship with life. When Karen Coffey encounters a ghost, she tells them, "I'm going to help you to where you need to go." Karen believes ghosts are similar to the negative of a photograph; they leave evidence, like a fingerprint. She considers being a paranormal is, "a double-edged sword." In some ways it's great to discover a spirit who inhabited a certain house; in other ways it's a curse to find out what she knows.

Karen shared another story. "In 1990, my son was born. When he was a little boy, I heard him chatting with someone. I thought he was watching television, but he said he was talking with someone I knew." It was Mikayla Luce, another granddaughter of Jonathan Luce. "My son described her as about his height. She would stand in the front hallway. The house has an open stairway. Apparently, Mikayla fell over the bannister down the stairs, broke her neck and died. She was the young woman my son spoke with." Karen's son and Mikayla Luce talked together for years.

The denouement of the story is intriguing. "A girl riding her bike up Centre Street saw a red ball in the graveyard behind town hall. She told me about it. It was my son's red ball. It was sitting on the grave of Mikayla."

"I had several different tenants at my house on 100 Centre Street. Some of the rooms were blocked off. There was a tenant there, during a storm, who felt a presence at the foot of her bed. It was a black woman, with a kerchief. She could have been a cook or a nanny for the sea captain who lived there." Karen pauses. "One time a broom flew across the room on the second floor."

*Ghosts are always in houses. It takes a particular person to discern them. It's reality. They're there.*

KAREN COFFEY NOT ONLY lived with ghosts at her home but also now works with one. Karen runs Pyewacket's on Beach Road. And yes, there's a ghost at Pyewacket's. His name is William Dugan, known as Babe. He died at the age of thirty-nine of cirrhosis of the liver. Karen has seen him in the building, smelled his pipe tobacco. Once, he called out her name, "Karen." Items in the store are moved about surreptitiously; that's how Babe attracts attention. Babe was a woodworker. In his nearby shop, he had a trap door where he would throw bottles. He died in 1963 and still haunts Pyewacket's.

A ghost is someone who has had an incomplete relationship. They don't know where they are, whether they're alive or a spectral sight. And Babe Dugan is still haunting Karen's shop.

Just down the street is the site where Mr. Feeney lived, a spirit who now haunts the area. Karen says the Feeney family once owned the Martha's Vineyard Campground. David Perzanowski, who runs Vineyard Scripts on the site of the old Feeney house, said, "The best I can do with Mr. Feeney is the noises we hear upstairs and we thought he turned OFF lights upstairs. We figured he was one of those thrifty old men watching his pennies."

David added a tale of a friend who photographed the West Chop Lighthouse one day. It appeared to empty. "When he looked at the picture later there was a woman in the window." Who was she? Where did she come from? Behind the door of every old house is a story, a history and perhaps a ghost.

# 9

# GHOST STORIES THROUGH THE YEARS

Sometimes we fool ourselves into seeing something that isn't there. Other times, we sense something isn't quite right, but it's fine. And then there are times, I understand, when we are receptive to the unknown. That's when a pretty unusual, but pretty neat, event occurs, and we're part of it, witnessing the unknown. Has that ever happened to you?

Early in the morning of November 21, 2019, about 5:45, I was on the road, driving to the Y for my spinning class. I've been attending the 6:00 a.m. class for years: it's early, energetic and exhilarating. This morning as I drove along the darkened street by the Oak Bluffs fire station, I witnessed what appeared to be an approaching vehicle, careening along the bike path, with uneven headlights; it was disconcerting, especially since I had begun to look into haunted experiences on Martha's Vineyard.

I proceeded slowly, keeping close to the right-hand side of the road. As I neared the approaching vehicle, I realized that in reality, it was two joggers, women running with headlamps, moving not quite in tandem, just a step off, which evoked the bouncing appearance of mismatched headlights. As I passed, I noted the back of their lamps were lit as well, in calming pastel colors that eased my angst.

No sooner had I breathed a sigh of relief and proceeded a little faster than I caught sight of an intense white orb directly ahead, a bright light shining right at me. Two more headlights were off to the left. All the lights were stationary, or so it seemed, but the very bright light was very disconcerting. I slowed down, grateful another car was in my lane, ahead of me, moving slowly.

The light was very bright. I slowed way down. The hairs on the back of my neck tensed up.

As I approached cautiously, I realized the bright light was a spotlight from a cruiser. A policeman had stopped a car for a traffic violation. Both vehicles were pulled to the side of the road; there was nothing really strange about the situation. It was totally normal.

I have never seen a traffic stop at 6:00 a.m. on County Road. On occasion I do pass a patrol car on my thrice weekly trips to the Y, pulled off to the side, facing the other way, lights off.

There were no ghosts about this morning, but I appreciated an intriguing and unusual experience as I drove to my spinning class.

~

We asked Hilary Wallcox, librarian of the *Vineyard Gazette*, to root through her files for any number of unusual events reported in the newspaper over the years.

The earliest spectral sighting and the only one reported in the first-person perspective was a tale related by Enoch C. Cornell in the spring of 1881. He was at Caleb's Pond, on Chappaquiddick, and experienced a strange sight. We reprint his tale in its entirety but cannot offer an explanation.

*May 7, 1881*

*Mr. E.C. Cornell, who spent the night of Friday last, with a companion at the Caleb's Pond herring fishery, relates the following:*

*Looking across the harbor in a south-west direction, at about midnight, there appeared midway of the plain an apparently well defined, square edged shaft of red-hot iron, which issued from the ground and ascended for about half a mile, at which elevation it remained for the space of about two seconds, and then vanished without explosion or other manifestation.*

*In about three or four seconds a second shaft, a perfect duplicate of the former, appeared, differing only in that it went up less than two thirds as high as the other, vanishing as before. This was followed by an illumination below, proceeding from no visible cause. It was raining slightly at the time, and pitch dark, except during the occurrence described, when the whole vicinity was brilliantly illuminated, so that woods and buildings were distinctly visible.*

Rereading this tale leads to no rational reason for these shafts of light to shoot up from Katama.

THE NEXT SERIES OF ghost stories were published in the spring of 1921, shortly after Henry Beetle Hough assumed ownership as editor of the *Vineyard Gazette*. We make that point because he made many changes in the operations and opinion of the newspaper and incorporated his unique vision in preserving the history and quality of life he found on Martha's Vineyard.

## April 28, 1921

This saga occurred by a cranberry bog along the Vineyard's north shore, near Cedar Tree Neck, one of the premier Sheriff's Meadow conservation sites. Back in the day, the bog was known as the Crying Swamp.

"Years ago," so the story goes, "even grown folks hurried past the place with a feeling of dread if they had occasion to be abroad in that vicinity after dark. To all the neighborhood the swamp was known as a queer, supernatural way."

The area was a wilderness, unkempt, forbidding and unwelcome. At night, it was especially frightening, a place no one wanted to have anything to do with.

The story continues: "Capt. Roland Luce, whose house was in the vicinity, was returning home one night from a social evening call. As he passed the swamp, the shrill cry of a child reached his ears. He listened and seemed to hear a baby wailing somewhere in the midst of the swamp."

Captain Luce was not afraid, but he did walk a little faster. Then he heard the sound again, a sad, long, wailing cry. And the sound was right behind him.

Rather than investigate, or even try to rescue the crying child, the good captain broke into a mad dash, losing his hat as he ran for home. Even as he ran, the mournful cries pursued him to his doorstep.

Captain Luce's race to the comforts and safety of his home was the first time the cries of the swamp had been heard. Afterward, a number of locals reported wails and cries emanating from the cranberry bog. Many heard the fearful sounds, and "for years the Crying Swamp was known and shunned after dark."

No one knew where the sounds came from or who emitted such fearful cries, often after dark, deep in the night and far, far away from people.

The newspaper report concluded, "At all events the Crying Swamp may still be pointed out to the inquisitive searcher, and many tales told of the wails which came forth on dark nights when nothing human could have given them voice." (For an explanation, check the letter to the editor at the end of this section.)

# May 5, 1921

"I once heard my mother tell of a man who was driving a yoke of oxen home through the woods behind Ram's Hill. He had been at work all day and was in a great hurry to reach home." If oxen are anything like horses, they know when they're headed home. That means food, so they generally will pick up their pace.

"But suddenly the beasts stopped. One of them roared and then the other. They bellowed and kicked, making a dreadful furor in the dark woods." The man driving the oxen did not know what to do. He tried to calm them. He urged them on. All to no avail.

Looking ahead, the teamster saw a man by the roadway. The man had no head.

"Frightened as he was, he spoke. As the headless spectre vanished into the woods, he called after him repeatedly but the ghost vanished or was lost in the gloom." The oxen stood motionless, shaking and quivering in the gloaming.

"The teamster doubted his sense, but his oxen stood trembling and shivering and they were as hot and as covered with sweat as if they had driven miles at a mad pace. That's when the storyteller asserts, 'I guess it was a ghost.'"

What makes this story unusual is that there is no reason for anything out of the ordinary to occur on this old roadway. There was no particular reason for the teamster and his oxen to be afraid, except when they saw the headless apparition along the roadway.

This report concludes with a curious comment: "It is also interesting that the first to notice the supernatural being were the oxen." Nothing indicated the teamster had any experience with the supernatural, with ghosts or any reason to suspect any pranks or misadventures in the area.

The final line of this piece puts the story in its proper perspective: "This is one of the outstanding ghost records of the Vineyard, for it offers little possibility of explanation and will probably remain a mystery."

# MAY 12, 1921

"The following, somewhat in line with the tales of the supernatural recently appearing in the *Gazette*, was told to the writer, a few years ago, by a resident of Gay Head, and is given for the benefit of others interested in the folklore of the Island."

This is a tale of two Native American wizards, each trying to out-do the other with their powerful magic and wizardly wonders. "Once upon a time there were two Indian wizards, who were rivals, each claiming to be more powerful than his fellow."

One wizard was a resident of Gay Head, while the other hailed from Menemsha. The wizard from the Head spent the day visiting his peer in Menemsha.

As evening fell, the Gay Head wizard said his good-byes and made preparations to leave. He had a long way to go and no horse.

"I can give you a horse," said the Menemsha wizard, picking up a piece of wood and handing it to the Gay Head wizard. "The visitor mounted the stick, which at once turned into a noble steed and bore him swiftly home."

A few days later, the wizard from Menemsha returned the visit by journeying all the way to Gay Head. When the time came for him to leave and head home, the Gay Head wizard said, "I am not so powerful as you, I cannot give you a horse, but I will give you a cane to help you on your way."

The moon shone through a crack in the wizard's home. The Gay Head wizard plucked a moonbeam, severed it from the moonlight, and passed it to the Menemsha wizard, who said, "You are greater than I, to have power over the moonbeams."

# MAY 19, 1921

## *The Winged Angel of Lambert's Cove*

This story is brief, but inexplicable. It took place near the shore of Lambert's Cove, a century ago. We do not know the protagonist or of any witness besides Mrs. X, who was considered "a particularly matter-of-fact person."

One day, Mrs. X happened to look out her kitchen window facing the nearby hills along the shore. She caught sight of an apparition, an image, drifting aloft, above the hills of Lambert's Cove. The vision was of a gorgeous woman, an angel perhaps, for the description included wings. The image floated over the hillside and eventually floated behind the hills and off out of sight. Mrs. X could not explain what had happened; she rubbed her eyes, followed the image, noted specific details and watched as it disappeared in the distance.

The *Gazette* description noted that the floating angel was "a beautiful woman in diaphanous robes and with a dazzling pair of gauze-like wings [who] was hovering, settling gently through the clear air." This ephemeral creature drifted off and was never seen again.

Who knows what this was? An unusual bird, a figment of Mrs. X's imagination or an angel? Without further data we have to accept it as an unknown experience by a woman who could not explain what she had seen.

A Dream? Ghostly? Ephemeral? We are left with no explanation of what was seen.

# MAY 21, 1921

*The captain of a whaleship which sailed out of Edgartown along with many others was as bold a sea dog as ever lived. In seamanship he was the equal of any man living. In battle he might have bested the most stouthearted foe.*

*His ship was at sea, when the crew was repeatedly frightened by blood-curdling yells. Some of the men were playing cards in the cabin when they were startled by the yells, and they threw their cards into the fire.*

The frightful sounds unsettled the crew; they were upset by the unseemly screeches. The captain realized he had to determine where the howls originated to calm his crew. "The captain determined to search the ship, for he did not believe in ghosts."

The captain set out in search of the creature or creatures making such unseemly yells. He trod cautiously deep down into the hold, into the very bowels of the ship. The yells and cries continued. The crew stayed back, frightened, afraid to follow. The captain made his way, farther and farther forward, finally reaching right into bow of the vessel.

The fear of the crew increased. "The yells occurred at frequent intervals and there was no apparent source from which they could be coming."

Clambering along on his hands and knees, the captain spied something that unnerved even this brave soul. His fear increased, and he was about to turn back when…

We end with a letter to the editor, dated May 7, 1937, to the editor of the *Vineyard Gazette*. We print the letter in its entirety, as it is well written and exposes how two of these frightening experiences were explained.

# MAY 7, 1937

## *Lot Rogers Laid the Ghost*

*To the Editor:*

*It seems a pity to spoil a good ghost story, but it so happens the favorite story of my childhood was one of how my great grandfather, Lot Rogers, laid the Crying Swamp ghost. None of the neighbors would go near the place at night unless it were a matter of urgent necessity, so great grandfather decided to do something about it.*

*I do not know whether he took with him a Bible or a stout oak stick, but out to the Crying Swamp he went on one of the wild windy nights that the ghost seemed to favor.*

*He soon heard in the distance the mournful wails that had struck terror to stout hearts. Following and listening, he came at last to the ghost, two branches growing so close that in a high wind they grated together with a screaming wailing sound that, alone in the woods on a dark night, might well be taken for something supernatural.*

*Great grandfather also disposed of a ghost on a haunted ship. Not long out of port, the crew were terrified by wild unearthly howls and moans that seemed to come from the hold. Sailors were superstitious folk in those days, and the voyage seemed doomed to disaster from the start.*

*So Lot Rogers took it upon himself to find out what it was all about. His shipmates protested vainly, so they tied a rope around him to drag him back from whatever demons might lurk in the hold, and he went down, bringing to light nothing worse than a four footed stowaway, in the shape of a hungry and terrified cat.*

*Susan G. Amidon*
Vineyard Haven

# MAY 6, 1949

## *"The Ha'nt of the Hollow as Reconstructed"*

The following tale was published in the spring of 1949. It bears the threats of a curse on a young home builder and a lasting impact on the building site.

Around the year 1800, a young man wanted to build himself a house in Chilmark. It was to be a two-story house, and he set to work, determined to construct a home for his family.

For some reason, a neighbor was angry at the builder for an unnamed action that infuriated her. The young man refused to correct the misdeed or change his ways. In retaliation, the neighbor put a curse on him, warning the builder that his ambition will be his undoing. She cursed the young man, as well as whoever lived there, forevermore. "The fruits of your ambition, and all which you possess in your sinful pride shall turn to dust in your mouth. It shall choke and smother you and yours and all who shall come after you."[43]

Accordingly, the property was, "ridden by a curse for many generations." Indeed, the curse has been "experienced by those who have attempted to live and do business in that place." The curse affected anyone who sought to use that property.

The young man completed building his house, but it turned out that "life was unpleasant in that house from the beginning." The curse caused sand to drift down from the ceiling. The plaster on the walls was poorly prepared, and dust was all about. The upshot was that the young man and his family moved out.

Other people tried to live in the house over the years but could not contend with the drifting sands and dust all around.

Although abandoned, the house was still standing around 1900. Sheep roamed through the yard. Bushes and brambles surrounded the property. No one dared assume ownership of the property. It was abandoned to natural decline.

On occasion, vandals or brave young children broke into the house and explored inside. The interior was covered with sand and very dusty. There was a hissing sound of drifting sand that frightened intruders away.

Even the brave souls who poked around the homestead searching for and picking blueberries were confronted with sand amid their berries. And when popped into pickers' mouths, the blueberries bore a gritty taste. The house has long since been torn down and the plot lost in the annals of history and mystery.

~

*It's almost Halloween. Vineyarders have just as much reason for observing the day as mainlanders. Tales of the supernatural are everywhere on the Island, if only you take the time to look. There are at least enough ghost stories on the Vineyard to keep both believer and disbeliever in debate. These tales are part of Vineyard history.*

Thus begins a column in the *Vineyard Gazette* that appeared days before Halloween. Each week, Hilary Wallcox, librarian of the files of the *Vineyard Gazette*, pores over the annals of the newspaper to prepare a column that recounts historical highlights from years gone by. With 175 years of documented history, Wallcox has no shortage of material for her weekly column.

Following are excerpts from a column prepared for Halloween, a timeless trove of tales to haunt those seeking a good night's sleep. We've already touched on some of these tales; others add another element to the haunting happenings on Martha's Vineyard.

"There is the Crying Swamp of the North Tisbury, a special place in the woods where folks say a special spirit resides." Hilary Wallcox further characterizes the protagonist: "A curmudgeon New Englander of Island blood, Captain Luce was not often shaken by sounds coming from the woods or sea. Still, Captain Luce was convinced that some supernatural character resided in the swamp."

Hilary describes the setting in detail, adding a sense of urgency to the mystery in the swamp. Her historical addendum brings the story up to date: "Years later the area was converted to a cranberry bog and has since been returned back to wild vegetation."

Our erstwhile librarian recounts another ghost story we've already encountered, "the tale of oxen being driven by a resident through a secluded wood in that area known in North Tisbury as Ram's Hill." Of course, dark storm clouds were on the horizon as night approached. "'Suddenly the oxen stopped in their tracks and began to quiver,' reported the *Gazette* in an April 30, 1937 article."

To maintain the tension of the tale in this eighty-plus-year-old article, it was reported that "suddenly he [the teamster] saw a strange and frightening sight. A headless figure moved out of the woods, along the road, and then vanished."

Back to our librarian, she notes that the story, most likely written by Joseph Chase Allen, points out: "The odd part of this occurrence was that the apparition was seen or sensed by the oxen before the driver was aware of it." And the piece concludes that "anyone who believed in ghosts may use this to bear out the view that there are some specters beyond the knowledge of man."

To put her column in a historical context, Wallcox added the specific detail that years ago, when the majority of Vineyarders were firm believers in ghosts, it was common practice to ward off spectral phenomena by painting the front door of the house a bright red. According to Gale Huntington, progenitor of the *Dukes County Intelligencer* (now the *Martha's Vineyard Museum Quarterly*), were one to scrape the paint off front doors of old Vineyard houses, one would encounter a layer of red paint.

The Halloween column concludes with a mysterious story of an old man who limps through the woods of Chappaquiddick. "He just appears, walks a little distance and vanishes into nowhere." Apparently, his mission is just to keep an eye on anyone who ventures on what was once known as the Jeremiah estate, on Chappaquiddick.

And the final ghost story is not a mystery at all.

An Edgartown woman, Hannah Smith (1789–1878), recounted a memory from her youth. Whil mulling over the wonders of the world, deep in thought, she meandered down a lane to a nearby pond and sat down, contemplating the beauty of nature.

In her journal, Hannah Smith recalled,

> *Full of reflection of this melancholy nature I gazed at the waters round me, and terror thrilled through every nerve. This is the hour, mused I, that ghosts are thought to leave their solitary dwellings and visit the nocturnal traveler as they stroll about the hills and valleys. Roused by these melancholy thoughts I hastily left my seat and pursued my route towards home.*

In short, Hannah Smith frightened herself, just by watching the waters around her. Her journal entry concludes, "As I approached the house, sounds of more than terrestrial melody stole on my ear. I made a step to see whence the sounds came. It was my father playing a melancholy air on his violin."[44]

VINEYARD CELEBRANTS OF HALLOWEEN are sometimes too quick to recite ghost stories from the mainland and not those of here. In the cold season ahead, Vineyarders needn't look too far to find something going bump in the night.

The night is dark. And it is Halloween. You are driving home from a party in Chilmark near Windy Gates when your car's engine suddenly and unexpectedly dies on a dark, quiet road. Attempts to restart it prove futile, and with no cellphone reception, you are forced to search for help. A faint light far off in the dense woods signals a flicker of hope for salvation, so you grab your flashlight and head out.[45]

Approaching a house off the road, as the drizzle becomes a heavier rainfall, you catch sight of a light in the window. A woman appears to dash by the light. Yet as fast as the light appears, it turns off. Still, you approach the house, intent on asking the homeowner if you can use a phone to call for help. The house no longer appears to be inhabited; the flitting woman is a figment of your imagination. Your flashlight flickers and dies.

"You hear the sound of glass shattering followed by what sounds like an old woman singing. Dropping the flashlight, you turn and bolt back from where you came."

And now the denouement: "If this scenario sounds like nothing more than your typical ghost story, well, it is." Author Max Hart has led us right onto the grounds of Windy Gates, building tension out of his imagination.

JIM HICKEY OFFERS HIS take on Halloween ghost stories:

> *Ghost stories are as common here around this time of the year as Black Dog T-shirts in the middle of August. And while many swear they have seen a Vineyard ghost, all the tales cannot be true. Someone by now would have filmed the ghostly horseman of Black Brook or dug up the treasure buried in the Great Plains which is allegedly responsible for the phenomenon known as the Katama Money Light.*[46]

After reprising a number of haunted happenings, Jim Hickey reverts to the tried and true, projecting his own perspective on what has happened or appears to happen on the Vineyard: "So I never actually saw a ghost down by the cliffs. But for me, there is no denying some type of cosmic energy engulfs the entire area—whether it be friendly or hostile."

# 10

# GEOLOGICAL ANOMALIES

*T*he *Story of Martha's Vineyard*, published in 1908 by the Hine Brothers, written by Charles Gilbert Hine and illustrated by Thomas Hine, contains a fascinating array of magical mysterious musings on Vineyard history. On the advice of Chris Baer, local high school teacher, author, historian and savant, we perused the pages to parse pieces relating to spectral experiences from years gone by.

We uncovered tales of pirates and buried treasure. There were Indian myths and legends. We found mention of the British on the Vineyard, both during the Revolution and the War of 1812. And we read of unusual adventures our Vineyard forebears overcame over the years. We share some of Hine's tales to augment our poltergeist adventures and suggest that whatever supernatural events are encountered in the modern era are no more unusual or untoward than those experienced generations ago.

The most intriguing aspects of Hine's little treasure are his examples of geographic anomalies and changes that have occurred over the years. He references disappearing islands, eroding shorelines, sunken forests and natural phenomena that have affected Martha's Vineyard, not just eons ago but within the span of Hine's nineteenth-century lifetime. Climate change and the effect of the raging rising ocean are detected, described and discussed and present the influence and whims of nature. While these natural events are not exactly haunted happenings, they are unusual, strange, mysterious and somewhat difficult to adequately understand and explain.

We begin with changes along the Vineyard shoreline. We know from Henry Whiting's 1850 map of Martha's Vineyard and David Foster's 2018 *Between Land and Sea* that Martha's Vineyard has experienced a great deal of erosion along its shorelines, especially along the South Shore. Hine's research expands the erosive impact of the ocean.

To assess geological evolution over the years, we start with Moshup, the legendary ancestor of the Native Americans. Moshup was the first to reach Martha's Vineyard, and as a giant, he simply plodded across the waters. "The fabled giant Moshup coming home after a long and weary tramp, dragged one of his heavy feet upon the ground, and that his great toe cut a deep channel to the sea which the tidal waters filled."[47] This legend neatly overlaps nineteenth-century Professor Shaler's belief that the Vineyard was once part of Cape Cod. Shaler argued that the Vineyard was cleaved from the Cape by river action along the south side of the Cape. This concept was augmented by David Foster's view that activity from the Cape Cod glacier and the Buzzard's Bay glacier, working independently, but in tandem, squeezed the Vineyard, all those years ago, creating the iconic inverted V shape at the north end of the island.

Charles Hine noted that local cartographer Henry Whiting mapped the Vineyard in the mid-1800s. Whiting documented that the bluff of East Chop had receded seventy-five feet in twenty-five years, or three feet a year. Hine calculated some thirteen million cubic feet of shoreline of soil and rocks were washed by strong currents around East Chop and into Vineyard Haven Harbor.

Soil and rock from East Chop formed the marshy barrier beach along the north shore of the lagoon, creating Eastville Beach by the drawbridge and the shoreline that forged the lagoon as a separate body of water. Hine makes the point that the opening to the lagoon occurred in a violent storm in 1815. The first drawbridge was not constructed until 1872, then linking Eastville with Vineyard Haven along Beach Road.

And Crystal Lake, aka Ice House Pond, on East Chop, presents a double-shoreline. Hine wrote, "The small fresh water pond, whose southeastern bank was once the harbor shore, while now the road travels the new made shore some hundreds of feet farther out."[48] In other words, the original shoreline was the inner side of Crystal Lake, and the extensive removal or erosion of earth and stones created the barrier now traversed by East Chop Drive. (Interestingly, early maps of East Chop depict a roadway as an extension of Crystal Lake Drive; remains of such a roadway are evident today.)

Charles Hine described natural currents that formed Crystal Lake with outwash from around East Chop. That's almost a spiritual explanation. *Painting by Susannah Haney.*

Similar activity to Crystal Lake and the lagoon is mirrored along Sengekontacket by State Beach. Professor Nathanial Shaler believed that the pond initially was a wide bay. A wall of sand, now known as State Beach, blocked Sengekontacket from the ocean. That broad beach of sand proved the nemesis of the Martha's Vineyard Railroad, as ocean water and sand destroyed sections of track each year. Of the road that runs along State Beach, Hine complained, "It is a good road, and consequently much affected by the automobile, whose indecent haste prevents its occupants from enjoying the view and fills the eyes and clothes of less rapid citizens with dust and distress." In those early days of the automobile, the author criticized vehicular traffic for spoiling the views and atmosphere along State Beach. The more things change, the more they remain the same.

BASS CREEK EXEMPLIFIES HOW Vineyard topography has changed in the not-so-distant past. Early ferryboats from Woods Hole to Vineyard Haven (then Holmes Hole) entered the harbor and proceeded down Bass Creek, a tidal estuary that flowed from the head of the harbor by the current Steamship Authority, along Water Street and Lagoon Pond Road, into the lagoon. The ferry docked by Five Corners for patrons to disembark.

Charles Banks, our venerated Vineyard historian, reported: "The frequent and natural choice of the locations of a tavern was at a ferry landing, and usually one person combined the duties of ferryman and innkeeper."[49] Seventeenth-century ferryman Isaac Chase sailed his sloop to Falmouth; he also ran a hotel in Holmes Hole. At the end of the day, he secured his boat on Ferryboat Island, the larger of two tiny islands in the waters at the head of the lagoon, in the shadow of the Martha's Vineyard Museum.

It is intriguing that Five Corners, the busiest intersection on island, was once where passengers debarked the ferry and that Bass Creek was the only entrance to the Lagoon. Bass Creek originally flowed along what we now know as Water Street, right past the current Stop & Shop building. The creek was over six feet deep in 1807.

Centuries ago, the predecessors of today's steamships would tie up at Ferryboat Island. Mother Nature made some spiritual changes to our environment. *Photo by Joyce Dresser.*

Bass Creek once flowed from the current Steamship Authority building in Vineyard Haven along Water Street and into the Lagoon. That was before haunting natural changes occurred. *Photo by Joyce Dresser.*

The Great September Gale of 1815 breached the barrier beach by the present Beach Road, creating an opening to the lagoon where the drawbridge is today. Bass Creek was superfluous; it was filled in. The ship *Zeno* was sunk in the creek in 1835; twenty years later, more of the creek was filled in to become the eponymous Water Street. Today, the remains of Bass Creek lie along Lagoon Pond Road, an area that still floods. And in the mid-twentieth century, Veterans Memorial Park was created by filling in the swampy area where Bass Creek once flowed, according to islander John Hughes.

SOME FOUR THOUSAND YEARS ago Martha's Vineyard was connected to Cape Cod by a land bridge. As the glaciers retreated, ocean waters rose, covering the land with melting glacial waters; oceans rose four hundred feet. Swirling, rising waters moved sediment and eroded shorelines. The coastal landscape changed dramatically. Today, oceans rise more than one-eighth of an inch per year.

We are aware that sometimes Chappaquiddick is attached to the Vineyard. And sometimes not. Chappy's insular status depends on if the barrier beach at Norton Point is breached. Men excavated a breach to create a passage in 1921 and 1937, and it was opened by a gale in 2007, yet the gap closed in April 2015. At the moment, Chappaquiddick is not an island.

Originally, Chappy was two islands: East Beach to the lighthouse and the rest of Chappy. A great storm in 1725 closed the gap, forging the land together.

Skiff's Island, a mile east of Chappy, has sunk below the surface, making it an unpredictable and occasionally deadly geological anomaly. In the 1880s, the island was 1,200 feet long, 4.5 acres in size. Plans for a summer hotel were underway until the island disappeared. The *Mertie B. Crowley* ran aground on Skiff's submerged shore in 1910. Skiff's rose again in the 1950s, large enough to land an airplane, but once more it is underwater.

When Squibnocket was open to the sea, Aquinnah (Gay Head) enjoyed a full ocean bay. Middens of seashells have been found on the shore of Squibnocket, remnants of Native American life along the ocean bay.

Sheep once grazed on Middle Ground, a fabled island off West Chop. It was a sandy shoal in the 1800s, later home to a sunken forest, according to geologist Nathanial Shaler. He explained that the ebb tide pushed sediment through the sound, eliminating the island.

A sunken forest was discovered in Holmes Hole Harbor in 1833, looking like a marsh with stumps of cedar trees. A similar forest was discovered off the north shore. In a letter from Chilmark in the 1867 *Vineyard Gazette*, "the statement is made that a sunken forest is found in the Sound where tops and branches of trees have been repeatedly taken up, and that this sunken forest extends far out among Nantucket's shoals." Sunken forests could damage small boats.

Submerged forests were discovered in Wintucket and Janes Coves off the Vineyard in the early twentieth century. It was believed that the remains of these bygone trees show how the land has shifted over the decades, according to Charles Hine, in his 1908 tome.

In the 1970s, a red maple stump—dated to the 1500s—was found sixty-five feet offshore in four feet of water off Lake Tashmoo. Scientist David Foster reported tree stumps submerged in peat, and some off Stonewall Beach were dated from ten thousand years ago.

What causes these geological changes? Was it an unknown force, poltergeists or prophets? Who moved our landscape around? Chris Baer cannot predict the future but emphatically states that new islands will be formed along the coast while others will disappear. The ocean is a fearsome, dramatic force.

IN 1818, A THEORY was advanced that the earth was hollow, and one could sail inside at either the North or South Pole. This concept inspired French novelist Jules Verne to pen his *Journey to the Center of the Earth* in 1864.

Edward Everett, a Massachusetts politician, ridiculed this theory, saying it was foolish. However, to prove his point, he said it was as crazy as if one were to sail to Holmes Hole and enter the center of the earth that way. By introducing Holmes Hole to the discussion, the idea was born that the opening at the axis of the earth was called Holmes Hole.

IN 1885, ALEXANDER GRAHAM Bell, born in Scotland, visited the Vineyard to research the cause for the deaf community on the island. (He became interested in the deaf, as both his mother and wife were deaf; that was the inspiration for his invention of the telephone.) While staying in Vineyard Haven, he learned of an explosion experienced by a number of cranberry pickers in a bog near Wilfred's Pond by Lake Tashmoo. The berry pickers became "startled by a loud volcanic sort of rumbling sound from the ground," according to a letter Bell penned to his wife. Water blew a dozen feet in the air, and a cloud of steam hung over the area before it dissipated. No one could explain what happened, but a modern scientist proposed that it was a "methane gas expulsion event," which occurs with a build-up of gas from organic matter.

# 11

# SEAFARING TALES

P irates! "On a dark and stormy night an unknown vessel dropped anchor in the surf."[50] So begins a pirate tale that took place off Wasque Bluff on Chappaquiddick. Pirates dug a hole in the beach near a bluish-tinted rock, buried a box and the captain tossed in a "small green package which, with a muttered invocation to the father of pirates, he threw on the box, when instantly with crash and roar a blinding, lurid flame of pale green shot out of the hole, and for a moment lit up all the country round." Then the hole filled in of its own accord.

The story continues, as a local man bore witness to this explosive escapade. Later, the man agreed to meet a friend at the site by the bluish stone. The man got there ahead of his comrade and lay down to rest. Soon he heard the noise of a ship approaching and saw a ship without a helmsman approaching the shore.

A number of skeletons appeared on the deck and debarked down a gangway, bearing a dead man they intended to bury. As they dug a hole, they struck an iron pot filled with gold and silver. The skeletons dumped the body atop the pot, then spied the witness, our local man, and came for him. He started to run, then stood his ground and screamed, and the skeletons boarded their ship and sailed away.

> *Some there be who claim that a stranger whose heel prints showed a curious cleft did secure the pot, and transported it and himself to unknown parts on a mysterious vessel that had been hovering on the horizon for days, and it may be so, for recent digging fails to cause any unusual disturbance, except possibly in the backs and muscles of the diggers.*[51]

ANOTHER PIRATE TALE OCCURRED on Quay's Neck by Eastville Beach in Oak Bluffs. Was treasure buried there? Around 1850, the whaleship *Splendid* paid the Vineyard a visit, setting two captains ashore.

Two ships had departed the Dutch East Indies. One ship was filled with gold but was wrecked in the Spice Islands. The crew of the second schooner rescued the gold. The captains of both ships plotted to steal the gold and conceal the theft.

The captains met up with the *Splendid* in the Indian Ocean. Together they transferred all the gold aboard that ship, then abandoned the other. The captains buried the gold near the opening to the lagoon, as there was no bridge there at the time. Later, the pirates dug up the cache and sailed off to Falmouth.

Of course, in any dramatic tale of pirates, it was a dark and stormy night, with the wind whistling and the rain pouring down. The (two captain) pirates tried to bury the gold in Falmouth, but a group of locals dug up the money and deposited it in the Falmouth bank, then arrested the two captains. Later stories claim the pirates took only half the gold out of the hole by the lagoon and the rest is there for the digging.

THERE IS A TALE of two men who buried a large bundle by a great rock on the shore of Lake Tashmoo. Word was the bundle contained the body of a member of the crew who died of smallpox; others thought it was buried treasure. Three treasure hunters sought to dig up whatever it was. When the first man began to dig, "the earth opened under his feet and he sank with a yell to his armpits, while all manner of uncanny noises came from out of the darkness."[52]

IN AUGUST 1815, TWO men appeared on the shore near Squibnocket. They requested to stay the night with Abner Mayhew. When they arose the next day, one man asked how far it was to the city of New York. When Abner told the men they were over two hundred miles away from the city, the men were astonished. They thought they were on the shore of Long Island and could easily walk to the Big Apple. So, instead, the men headed to Menemsha and hired a boat to take them to New Bedford.

These events faded into the past, "when there came a story to the Vineyard of a dying sailor who had confessed that he and others coming from the south on a brig carrying considerable specie, had conspired with the mate to murder the captain, passengers and crew, scuttle the vessel and escape with the gold in a small boat to the shore."[53] The pirates buried most of their treasure near Squibnocket, then headed to New Bedford.

Time passed. The pirate tale faded into fables shared around a campfire. Then one day, two strangers walked up to Abner Mayhew's house, on the shores of Squibnocket, the same house the New York pirates had visited, years ago.

The two men claimed to be naturalists, searching for unusual marine curiosities. Interestingly, they performed all their searching and discoveries at night. Then they abruptly left the Vineyard. Next day when locals visited the ground nearby, they discovered, to no one's surprise, a gaping hole along the shore. The pirates had retrieved their buried treasure.

EVERYONE LOVES TO FIND money. My stepson Christopher was swimming off State Beach one day. He reached out and plucked a dollar bill from the waves. What are the chances?

Way back in 1833, events conspired to create a tale about digging for money on Martha's Vineyard. The story described three young men working on a Katama farmer's field, plowing and removing stones in preparation for planting. During their labors, the plowshare coughed up a couple of silver coins. The first young man quickly snatched up the coins and pocketed them. The second man witnessed the take and switched places. He, too, pocketed some found money.

The two farming interns decided to split their newfound profits, leaving out the third member of the team. According to the press report in the *New Bedford Gazette*, "What they obtained no one can exactly state—but it is believed not far from two or three thousand dollars were excavated. This was divided between the two; leaving [out] the man in the field with them."

Apparently, the story was advanced that the silver coins had been buried in the Katama field by Captain Kidd. This is the only verified tale of finding buried treasure on the Vineyard. However, myriad tales abound of the possibility of pirates and buried money across the Island. In 1890, it was generally believed by most people on the Vineyard that the legendary Captain Kidd had buried his ill-gotten treasure on the island of Chappaquiddick. According to the *New York Evening Post*, if one were to dig out a hole some forty feet below the surface, it would lead to a trunk with the inscription of Captain Kidd.

Chris Baer reported on one zealous treasure-hunter:

> *A rather fancifully written 1896* Boston Globe *story reported that Gay Head residents had "no doubt" that Captain Kidd buried "tons" of gold coins in kettles and oak barrels in the Cliffs and along the shore. When one zealous cliff digger, inspired by a supernatural vision, refused to stop digging when politely requested, "the man was taken bodily from the cliffs and carried down to the water's edge; this was repeated three times."*[54]

The obsession with a search for gold, whether hidden by Mother Nature or Captain Kidd, knows no bounds.

WHEN BRITISH SOLDIERS RAIDED Edgartown in the War of 1812, a local woman, Mrs. Swazie, proved clever enough to deceive the marauding British soldiers and save her family funds. Mrs. Swazie invited the redcoats in for tea, bringing them in through the front door and exiting the same, thus avoiding the spot by the side door where her husband had buried the family's valuables.

IN THE BATTLE OF Hedge Stakes in the War of 1812, a United States coasting schooner ran aground off Highland Beach. A British man-o-war was nearby. The British ship advanced, intending to rob the stranded schooner. Word reached farmers on shore. They joined forces aboard the stranded ship, armed with pickets or stakes from a nearby fence. As the British ship approached, the locals assaulted them. The American vessel was saved.

Because the men of this era were accustomed to both farming and sailing, they overcame the British, using the fence posts to assault the enemy. Never underestimate a local protecting his homeland.

ALSO DURING THE WAR of 1812, Captain David Smith returned to the island with a shipload of provisions for his inn. As he sailed around West Chop and into Vineyard Haven Harbor, he was accosted by two boatloads of British regulars. Captain Smith and his son rapidly sailed down through the renowned Bass Creek, now known as Water Street, and made their way safely through Five Corners and into the lagoon. Although British soldiers started firing at the captain and his son, a woman upstairs in a nearby house began to shoot at the British soldiers. Her fire repelled the soldiers, and Captain Smith survived.

THE AMERICAN SAILING SHIP *Hero* escaped the British privateer *Sir John Sherbrook* off No Man's Land during the War of 1812.

British vessels impounded American sailors and blockaded American ships, imposing an embargo, effectively preventing ships from sailing to Europe, sanctioning the United States, during the war. It was gratifying to read that an American ship outperformed a British ship in this needless war.

DURING THE WAR OF 1812, a British man-o'-war approached Squibnocket beach. Joseph Mayhew gathered neighbors, who hid along the shore and started to fire at the approaching boat. They managed to shoot some of the crew. It appeared to the British that a large number of men were along the shore, and the ship withdrew, heading to Gay Head, where it ran aground in the fog on the Peaked Rocks. A brass cannon was found in the waters, stuck to an anchor, deemed part of the British invasion.

~

AT THE START OF the Civil War, Union forces designed what was called the Anaconda Plan: sever Confederate supplies from East Coast ports and blockade Confederate ships from use of the Mississippi River. An anaconda is a snake that strangles its victims; such was the Union plan.

An example of the Anaconda Plan was the Stone Fleet. The Stone Fleet consisted of dozens of old or disabled whaling and cargo ships. At the end of 1861 and early 1862, more than thirty such ships were filled with stone and sailed down to Charleston South Carolina. They were intentionally sunk in the harbor to disrupt and blockade supply ships from England. (The South shipped cotton overseas in return for munitions.)

The plan was a bust. Confederate mariners steered their vessels around the sunken ships. The Rebels, however, were outraged at this blatant attempt by the North and vowed economic retribution.

Marylander Raphael Semmes served the United States as secretary to the lighthouse board from 1859 to 1861. During one of his national lighthouse surveys, he took a room, boarding with the Osborn family of Edgartown, prominent in the whaling industry. One of the leading captains was Abraham Osborn.

When war came, Semmes sided with the Confederates. He assumed command of the Confederate raider *Alabama*. Semmes proceeded to attack Northern whaleships and merchant vessels across the Atlantic. "And fate decreed that the paths of the one-time friends should again cross, though under very different circumstances."[55]

Semmes's first target was the *Ocmulgee*, a whaleship under captain Abraham Osborn. With cannon prominently on display, Semmes demanded the *Ocmulgee* surrender to his *Alabama*. Osborn had no choice, as his only weapons were harpoons. Semmes took the whalemen aboard ship and sank the *Ocmulgee*, imposing economic angst on the North but not inflicting injury to any whalemen.

When *Ocmulgee* was boarded, both crew and captain were taken prisoner. "Osborn, of course, had no idea who was in command of his captor, and his surprise can safer be imagined than expressed when he was confronted with Semmes, who no doubt was equally surprised at the identity of this his first victim, for the *Ocmulgee* was the first prize taken by the rebel cruiser."[56]

Semmes went on to sink sixty-five Northern commercial ships over nearly two years, capturing sailors and supplies. The Rebel cruiser *Alabama* was eventually sunk by the Union gunship *Kearsarge* in the English Channel, off Cherbourg, France, in June 1864.

However, the grudge the South felt about the Stone Fleet lingered.

Another vessel, the steam-powered armored cruiser *Shenandoah*, was outfitted in Liverpool and set sail late in 1864 under Confederate captain James Waddell. Again, the target was Northern merchant ships and whaleships, now hunting whales primarily in the Pacific. Captain Waddell was more aggressive than Captain Semmes, as he sailed across the seas in search of his prey.

Eventually, the Civil War ended with General Lee's surrender at Appomattox Court House, Virginia, on April 9, 1865. President Lincoln was assassinated a week later.

Captain Waddell of the *Shenandoah* did not get word that peace had been declared. He continued to capture and sink whaleships throughout the spring of 1865, well after the war was over. In June, he sank a half-dozen ships. Then he was officially informed the war was over. He didn't believe it and continued his marauding ways. In the late summer of 1865, he was shown a newspaper that proclaimed the war was over.

Captain Waddell could no longer claim ignorance; he was declared a pirate. During over a year of raids, Captain Waddell and his *Shenandoah* sank thirty-eight ships.

Late in November, the *Shenandoah* returned to the River Mersey, in Liverpool, and surrendered. Thus did the last Confederate flag fly during the Civil War.

The final denouement to this tale is that today, Captain Bob Douglas of Black Dog fame, has two sailing ships in Vineyard Haven harbor. The names of the vessels are the *Shenandoah* and the *Alabama*. What are the odds that those two ships were not named after the Southern raiders that sailed the seas, inflicting fear on whalemen all over the globe during and after the Civil War?

CHRIS BAER SHARES A number of sea serpent sightings in Vineyard waters. In July 1827 off Gay Head, a Captain Coleman, aboard his sloop *Levant* en route from Nantucket to the Connecticut shore, saw what he considered an infamous sea monster. Passengers and captain claimed they had a clear view of the creature, which bore a horse-like head and breathed through its nostrils. Its body was barrel shaped and more than sixty feet long.

Sea monsters were seen off the shore of Gay Head. Do you believe that? *Photo by Joyce Dresser.*

Seventy years later, en route from Boston to Baltimore, the crew and passengers of the steamer *Gloucester* reportedly encountered a serpent off Gay Head. This white creature was more than forty feet long with a body like a giant eel, about six inches around, with tapered head and tail. Chief Officer Walter Eldridge reportedly told the local newspaper that until this recent experience, he didn't believe in sea serpents and had never seen one. Now he was a confirmed believer.

And in 1930, a Captain Colwell aboard a trawler off Gay Head saw a yellow sea serpent more than fifty feet long. It had four small legs, its tail had ridges and the head was akin to a cow. The report noted the creature pushed against the bow of the vessel with a hind foot, to avoid a collision.

BEAR OR APE? WELCOME Tilton (1856–1949) saw something like a bear in the summer of 1915. It had a big round head and prominent white teeth and seemed to walk erect. Another man saw a similar-looking creature near his henhouse at night, shortly after the first sighting. The local said the footprints were like those of a child. A third incident occurred on North Road; the bear or whatever had big white teeth and a long tail and was spotted lumbering along. No other sightings or reports of such a creature turned up.

BOZZY WAS AN ALLIGATOR who lived in the Barnacle Club in Vineyard Haven. Bozzy was thirteen when he arrived in 1918. He was two feet long and enjoyed lolling around in a vat of warm water and having his stomach and throat scratched by caregiver George Fisher. A second alligator, Dickie, arrived in 1921 and two more the next year. There is no word what became of them when their caregiver passed away in 1923.

A PRIVATE HOSPITAL FOR mariners in Vineyard Haven was in operation prior to the Marine Hospital. One patient was a very sick sailor about to die. The undertaker was summoned; however, he was hard of hearing. Unfortunately, he went into the wrong room, the room where a nurse's son was sleeping soundly. The undertaker prepared the somnolent son for burial, "during which proceeding Ben slept peacefully on." The undertaker was so proud of his work he summoned Becky to the room. When she saw her son, she was so overcome she burst into tears. With that, Ben woke up, and the undertaker did what he was supposed to do in the first place.

IN THE FOLLOWING TALE, we're not talking about ghosts but a true story that could have spawned a spectral scene.

The year was 1866. Winter. The schooner *Christina*, from Yarmouth. Maine, laden with cement, was caught by a nor'easter off Chappaquiddick. The ship ran aground on Hawes Shoal and sank on January 7. The vessel was seen from shore, with crew clinging to the rigging. It was too cold, too choppy and too windy to execute a rescue. For three days, a rescue was postponed.

Finally, on January 11, a rescue boat made its way out to the *Christina*. The sole survivor of the six-man crew was Charles Tallman, the mate. His fingers and toes were severely frostbitten; he attributed his survival to a rubber overcoat.

Tallman was transported to Holmes Hole, where he was cared for over a period of weeks, but most of his digits had to be amputated due to frostbite. Tallman lost full use of his limbs and could have faded away as a nonentity.

Instead, Charles Tallman began life anew.

The *Vineyard Gazette* recognized Tallman as "one of nature's noblemen," and he assumed a new career, selling peanuts to tourists in Cottage City. Like Nancy Luce in West Tisbury, Tallman promoted himself with photographs and notes about the dramatic shipwreck. The Oak Bluffs Land & Wharf Company built him a little stall in Ocean Park to sell his peanuts, and he became a prominent fixture in the community.[57]

THE SHIP *CITY OF Columbus* left Boston on a cold and wintry night in midwinter 1884, bound for Savannah, Georgia. There were 132 passengers and crew aboard, steaming around Cape Cod, heading for Vineyard Sound. Passengers enjoyed a delicious dinner in an elegant dining room before heading off to their berths.

The ship was off course as it made its way into Vineyard Sound. The helmsman, rather than using the Gay Head lighthouse as a warning beacon, followed incorrect compass readings, which sent him away from the middle of the channel.

Whether it was failure to follow orders or inept seamanship, the *City of Columbus* ran aground on a massive submerged erratic, an undersea boulder known as Devil's Bridge, and it scraped the hold of the ship. The hull of the ship was torn open; ocean water rushed in. It was 3:00 a.m., and passengers, awakened by the lack of motion, sought safety in lifeboats already damaged beyond repair.

That night, 103 people drowned.

The passenger manifest bore the names of Mr. and Mrs. Chase, from South Newmarket, New Hampshire. Booked in State Room A, they never had a chance to survive. Like the *Titanic* a quarter century later, poor management of a disaster resulted in many lives lost.

Far away in New Market, New Hampshire, the father of one of the passengers, Nathaniel Bunker, awoke, screaming, from a nightmare. His recently married daughter was aboard the *City of Columbus*. Bunker knew, instantly, his daughter had drowned.

Nathaniel Bunker dreamed he stood on a high cliff, looking down at a great ship as it began to sink. The next morning, he told two friends of his nightmare: "I could see men, women and children struggling in the water. Wreckage was everywhere, and I saw Lou Chase trying to help my daughter into a lifeboat, but a big wave came and swept everything away."

Later, when news came over the telegraph, Bunker said he was already aware he would never see his daughter again. Had she sent a message in her dying moment?

IN 1928, THE STEAMSHIP *Nobska* was renamed *Nantucket*, and the *Islander* was renamed the *Martha's Vineyard*. During an especially rough ride aboard the *Nobska/Nantucket*, a luggage rack, filled with gravestones en route for use on the Vineyard, started rolling back and forth across the freight deck, spooking the crew.

Fortunately, not one of the frightened steamship crew needed his own gravestone as a result of this runaway freight cart.

~

OSCAR PEASE JOINED THE U.S. Army in World War II, intent on serving his country by helping to halt the Nazi invasion of Europe. In 1944, he was aboard a transport ship heading to France. The ship was painted a typical battleship gray, with a red cross on it. Oscar Pease felt an eerie sense of familiarity with the vessel.

As the Chilmark soldier meandered around the ship, he realized why the vessel felt so familiar: it was the Vineyard ferry *Naushon*, appropriated by the U.S. Navy to serve as a transport and hospital ship in the Normandy invasion. Oscar Pease felt right at home. "As he recounted it, the ship was fog-bound during the crossing. And yet the ship was familiar. He knew where the companionway way; he did not need directions. He was overcome, he said, by an eerie sense of familiarity."[58]

The story related by Oscar Pease was confirmed by Jimmy Morgan, renowned Menemsha swordfisherman. As reported by Phyllis Mearas for *Martha's Vineyard Magazine*, Morgan shared his recollection of an encounter with a Vineyard ferry on the other side of the Atlantic Ocean:

> We also went into Cherbourg, France, and when we got there, they were calling for volunteers to go to the train station to carry the stretchers with the soldiers on them who had been in the Battle of the Bulge. There in Cherbourg, I saw a familiar vessel tied up. She was the Naushon, one of our Island steamers that had been turned into a Red Cross hospital ship.[59]

The *Naushon* transported the first casualties of Normandy across the English Channel in June 1944. Morgan recalled, "I was on a Liberty ship. She had a red cross painted on her; white with a red cross. She was a hospital ship." How did he know for sure it was the *Naushon*? "I knew it was her right off, from her profile. We knew all the steamers in those days, the *Martha's Vineyard* and the *Nantucket*." Of the *Naushon*, Morgan recalled, "She was more elaborate."[60]

BUDDY VANDERHOOP HAS BEEN fishing off Gay Head for decades. He knows the ocean waters like the back of his hand and has every confidence in getting around the Gay Head peninsula. Yet he recounts an experience that happened a few years ago that was so spiritual, so unreal, so inexplicable, that it bears re-telling.

Buddy was in charge of retrieving the remains of Native Americans and returning them to the Vineyard for proper burial. One evening, he set out from New Bedford with the skeletal remains of a mother and two infant daughters. Their remains had been stored in the basement of the Peabody Museum. Vanderhoop's responsibility was to return the bodies to the Vineyard for proper interment.

The night was dark and foggy, yet Buddy Vanderhoop was confident he knew where he was and where he was going. He set off steaming across Vineyard Sound. It was a moonless night, with nary a twinkle of a star or a ship's beacon to combat the poor visibility. As Buddy headed to the Vineyard, he felt proud of his cargo, proud to be a Native American, proud to care for his ancestors.

> *En route, in the middle of Vineyard Sound, Mr. Vanderhoop experienced a strange aura, a sense that something was amiss. Lacking radar or a searchlight, he slowed his boat to ascertain why he felt such a strange sensation. As he reduced engine speed, a great freighter passed right across his bow. Had he not paused at that moment, "all of us would have gone down," he said. It was a traumatic moment. He felt the spirits of the deceased guided him through this crisis.*[61]

Captain Vanderhoop was shaken. Why had he slowed his vessel? Something, somewhere led him to believe he was in danger, and Buddy believes it was the guardian spirits of his ancestors who saved his life that night.

AND WE END THIS section with a couple of most mysterious propositions.

## ON BARTHOLOMEW GOSNOLD

Bartholomew Gosnold was the first white man to settle on Martha's Vineyard, although his 1602 settlement on Cuttyhunk lasted only six weeks. Gosnold and his crew built a fort and planted crops, then returned to England. Did Gosnold's ship ever return? Apparently, spectral sightings have occurred over the years.

> *On May 25, 1902, a Vineyard fisherman anchored at Cuttyhunk observed a thunderstorm swirling up out of the northwestern sky. Through the murky mists, he beheld an old bark with a crew of transparent sailors and a transparent captain. The fisherman hauled up anchor and fled for home.*[62]

According to legend, Bartholomew Gosnold's phantom ship appears annually off Cuttyhunk. While we cannot vouch for more sightings, a historical anomaly is worth looking into.

Did anyone from Gosnold's short-lived settlement in 1602 remain on island, making them the first white men on Martha's Vineyard? Poor planning in the original expedition left inadequate supplies to maintain the settlement beyond six weeks in 1602. Gosnold had to return to England. However, there was not enough food for the whole crew. Gosnold was in a quandary.

Whether Gosnold sailed with a full crew or some remained on Cuttyhunk, we don't know. "Could the first English settlers on the Vineyard have arrived with Bartholomew Gosnold himself in 1602?"[63]

In his Pease Tradition treatise, A.C. Trapp proposed that "English settlers were already living on Martha's Vineyard when the Mayhews arrived in 1642," according to editor Bow Van Riper. "The island must have been one of the most desirable locations in all of the English claim to the New World at the time."

Two crew members, Archer and Brereton, kept logs of the voyage. "It would seem that the consensus of opinion is that Gosnold did leave behind some men on one of the islands near Martha's Vineyard," wrote Trapp in 1986. Supplies were scarce; survival was in question. Brereton wrote of "leaving this island with as many true sorrowful eyes as were desirous to see it."[64]

Trapp assumed eight people remained, perhaps wives and children with the names Browning, Norton, Vincent, Trapp and John Pease. If this theory could be proven, it would mean their descendants have a longer lineage on Martha's Vineyard than any Mayhew. And that would be a story worth looking into.

# 12

# MURDER, SHE WROTE

*Murder, She Wrote* was Angela Lansbury's renowned television show that ran from 1984 to 1996. Based on the Agatha Christie novel *4:50 from Paddington, Murder, She Wrote* was a detective drama led by fictitious writer Jessica Fletcher. Like the television series, people who love ghost stories are drawn to murders—and often ghosts are connected with an untimely death.

On the Vineyard, we cannot directly tie any of the following murders to a ghost, but the actual murder stories are worth reviewing. Perhaps a reader will make a connection or find a link between one of these horrible tales and something more spectral.

Over the years, a small number of people have been murdered on Martha's Vineyard. That's a good thing. And because that number is so small, it is worth investigating; most often, if the death occurred in unusual circumstances, there is an opportunity for a poltergeist to make an appearance.

Murders have an attraction simply by their horror: what is worse than getting murdered? There is a spiritual concern with meeting an untimely death: ghosts continue to struggle with the repercussions of a frightful demise during the lifetime. Many of the tales we have read are founded on someone's death that occurred in a disastrous, unusual or unpleasant manner. We look at a few prominent murders on the Vineyard over the years.

BEING ON A SMALL boat in the middle of the ocean can be a claustrophobic experience. Being aboard a whaleship with a ruthless murderer would be a frightful situation. A pair of nineteenth-century mutinies are worth exploring to grasp the drama and fear of men in tight spaces over a long time under unpleasant conditions.

The whaleship *Globe* set sail from Edgartown on December 15, 1822, under the command of Captain Thomas Worth (1793–1824), reputed to be a strict disciplinarian. One member of his crew, Samuel Comstock, from Nantucket, served as boatsteerer and harpooner, a key officer aboard a whaleship.

Comstock sought to become king of a South Seas island and viewed his term aboard the *Globe* as a means to that end.

Conditions aboard the *Globe* were not promising. After months at sea, few whales had been captured, rations were poor and several sailors deserted ship. Two members of the crew kept journals that attested to the conditions.

On January 26, 1824, Comstock and two accomplices used a hatchet to kill Captain Worth and shoot two officers. The *Globe* put in at a south sea island so Comstock and his cohorts could realize his dream. Within a relatively short time, natives murdered all of them. So much for Comstock's dream.

Altogether thirteen shipmates were killed, seven of them Vineyarders. It was the most murderous mutiny in the history of whaling. Gilbert Smith and five surviving crew escaped and were rescued nearly two years later. News of the mutiny filtered out slowly; residents of the Vineyard and Nantucket heard of the crime, but not the details.[65]

The *Globe* returned to port in November 1824. Incidentally, Major General William Jenkins Worth (1794–1849), brother of Thomas, proved a hero years later in the Mexican War. Worth planned a number of forts along the Texas frontier and led the Department of Texas in 1849. Worth died of cholera at the age of fifty-five. Fort Worth, Texas, is named for him.

CAPTAIN HOWES NORRIS OF Eastville, Oak Bluffs, was an experienced whaleman. He set off in command of the *Sharon* on May 25, 1841, following a route similar to the *Pequot*, the imaginary ship under Captain Ahab: sailing around the Cape of Good Hope and Indian Ocean to the Pacific. (The story of *Moby-Dick* parallels the tragedy of the *Sharon*; Herman Melville wrote his masterpiece shortly after the account of the *Sharon* surfaced.)

Captain Norris, often drunk, began to beat members of the crew for small infractions. Over time, he focused his anger on the cook, George Babcock, a Black man.

Nine crew members deserted ship at Grenville Island; a couple of Hope Island natives were enticed to sign on as replacements. Two members of the crew kept journals. Third mate Benjamin Clough recorded that Norris beat and starved Babcock over the summer of 1842. On September 1, Babcock died and was buried at sea.

Few whales were captured, rations were low and more men deserted. On November 6, "the Hope Islanders, fearing for their own lives, and armed with a cutlass and a cutting spade, brutally attacked and killed the captain."[66]

Two whaleboats were off chasing a whale. They learned of the mutiny when the cabin boy hoisted an inverted flag atop the mainmast. The crew in the whaleboats feared the *Sharon* would sail away, abandoning them seven hundred miles from land.

That night, Benjamin Clough leapt out of the whaleboat and swam back to the *Sharon*. Covertly, he clambered aboard, overpowered the two islanders and ushered back the two whaleboats. The *Sharon* returned to New Bedford on February 10, 1845, satisfactorily loaded with whale oil. Clough was promoted to master on his next journey.

Later in his career, Benjamin Clough endured episodes with both cannibals and ice floes. Cannibals threatened Clough and his men on one of the Pacific Islands. His life was threatened in the Arctic Ocean by ice floes that pulled him underwater. Another dangerous incident occurred when his harpoon line got tangled around his leg and he was pulled underwater by a whale. Miraculously, he was able to escape all these situations.

Marston Clough, a great-grandson of Benjamin Clough, is a prominent Vineyard artist. He and his brothers recall their ancestor's bravery and courage.

During a severe thunderstorm in 1851, lightning streamed down the chimney in the house of Elwina Norris, widow of Captain Norris. The lightning struck her in the ear, killing her instantly. The flash was so hot it melted the hands on the clock and the andirons in the fireplace. After the storm, a heavy cloud hovered menacingly over the town of Holmes Hole.

Howes Norris Jr., son of the captain and Elwina, was editor of the *Cottage City Star*. He became an ardent secessionist for Cottage City when voters at town meeting severed ties with Edgartown in 1880. (Cottage City became Oak Bluffs in 1907.)

～

JUST BEFORE CHRISTMAS, ON December 23, 1863, a local shopkeeper, William Luce, was brutally murdered in Holmes Hole. The culprit was never captured. The crime lingers on the books, unsolved.

No one knows why William Cook Luce, son of Jonathan Luce, was brutally slain in his grocery and dry goods store by the Steamship Authority building in Vineyard Haven. His wallet was later found on the street. The murderer killed Luce with a hatchet yanked off the wall of his store. To make sure he was dead, the assailant sliced his throat. And no one witnessed the crime.

One potential witness did see three men walking up Union Street from the harbor. The men were boisterous and obnoxious, most likely drunk. They paused before the store and went inside. The man who saw them, one John Lewis, did not think anything of it until the next day, when the news of the murder surfaced.

At the time, in the midst of the Civil War, Holmes Hole Harbor was often filled with transient sailors ashore from ships sailing through Vineyard Sound. No concerted effort was launched to locate any miscreants, and within days, any and all possible suspects were no longer around.

Townspeople were frightened to have an unsolved murder in their midst.

Rumors floated about that Captain Gustavus Smith of Holmes Hole was guilty of the crime. Smith exhibited behaviors that made him appear liable for the murder. He sought assistance in caring for his ailing wife. And he displayed a misunderstood sense of humor regarding the murder of Luce, which some people interpreted as guilt.

Thus, this local man was charged with the crime. He was indicted on June 1, 1864, and spent five months in the Edgartown jail, under jailkeeper Samuel Daggett, before he was brought to Taunton, to face a judge.

*The denouement was perfectly ironic. Writing nearly fifty years later, [Smith's] attorney Stetson recalled that "The old jailer, Daggett, nearly eighty years old and almost blind, had a lot of trouble getting across the tracks and through the frisky locomotives at Taunton and never could have succeeded had not Captain Gustavus taken him by the shoulders and steered him as you would a wheelbarrow." There were hundreds at the depot to see "the Vineyard murderer" arrive. Naturally the crowd thought Daggett was the criminal, and that the hale, stout captain was the constable in charge.*[67]

Smith was found innocent and freed. His wife died, and he went back to sea. Gustavus Smith lived five more years, dying on the coast of Maine in 1869. The death of William Cook Luce, shopkeeper of Vineyard Haven, was never solved.

~

IN 1904, A WEALTHY bachelor farmer on Chappaquiddick traveled to New Bedford and brought back a woman he planned to marry.

Charles Pease, age forty-two, was held in high esteem by his Chappy neighbors and four sisters. The Edgartown populace considered Pease to be upstanding and of high character. He was industrious, prosperous and a confirmed bachelor.

The unexpected marriage took place on Saturday, April 30. No one knew where Pease had met his bride. Her name was Selma Larson, and she was about thirty, a schoolteacher from Norwood, of Swedish heritage. One day he went off island and returned with her. They were married in Edgartown.

Pease and his new bride spent several days savoring his farmlands that extended across Chappaquiddick. The couple was seen together, and Mrs. Pease intimated she planned to teach her new husband the game of golf.

Mid-week, May 4, Pease was found shot to death in a grove not far from his house. While the *Vineyard Gazette* claimed the death was a suicide, that was ruled out due to the location the long .44-caliber gun was found and how Mr. Pease had fallen when he was shot.

The new bride was heartbroken.

Earlier in the week, an unknown vessel had been seen offshore, lingering nearby for several days. Shortly after the murder, both the yacht and the bride disappeared. No one knew where the yacht and the new bride came from or where they went.

It was determined, by both the police and the press, that a former suitor of the bride had tracked down the couple to Chappy, slain Charles Pease, then absconded with the woman. No other outcome made sense.

Tisbury's Karen Coffey, a paranormal, walked in Pease's field on Tom's Neck. She found a broken metal chain that held energy. She knew the wife killed her husband (who had been shot in the mouth) then disappeared. "He treated her like a slave," said Karen. Perhaps the abrupt adjustment from a fancy lifestyle to farmer's servant was too much for her.

~

ON JULY 27, 1916, a bundle was seen floating in Farm Pond, Oak Bluffs. It turned out to be the body of thirty-six-year-old Henrietta McLeod of Milton, Massachusetts. She had recently been fired from her position as a cook for a family and was thought to be leaving the island. Instead, her body turned up in Farm Pond.

At first, McLeod's death was deemed a murder, and suspects were questioned. On further investigation, her demise was determined to be suicide.

~

THE PREMISE OF THIS next story is that an artist assumed the spirit of a deceased predecessor. Robert Swain Gifford (1840–1905) was a prominent maritime artist, born on Nonamesset, the easternmost Elizabeth Island, across from Woods Hole. His work hangs in the Smithsonian and the Metropolitan in New York.

Frederic Thompson (1868–1933) grew up in New Bedford and worked as an engraver in both silver and gold. He married a glass decorator, and the couple relocated to New York City, where Thompson worked for Tiffany & Company.

Robert Swain Gifford passed away in 1905. A few months later, Frederic Thompson visited the American Art Gallery. There he claimed Gifford requested that Thompson paint in Gifford's style; Thompson complied. Over the course of a year, Thompson painted a number of prominent works of art in the style of Swain Gifford.

A spiritualist, Dr. James Hyslop of the American Society for Psychical Research, was impressed by Thompson. Hyslop met with mediums who were convinced that Thompson channeled the deceased painter Gifford. Once the press got wind of this dichotomy, Thompson made a name for himself.

*Scene at Cuttyhunk* by Frederic Thompson was painted in 1908 and hangs in the Edgartown library. "This innocuous landscape belies a colorful Chilmark artist with a curious and convoluted story involving ghosts, poisonings, secret codes, hidden chambers, and the Mafia."[68]

According to spiritualists who communicated with Gifford after his death, the deceased artist was ecstatic that Thompson would complete his work. Thompson went on to become well known, painting impressionist

When the spirit of one artist migrates to another, this painting by Frederic Thompson, titled *Cuttyhunk*, is the result, hanging in the Edgartown Library. *Courtesy of the Edgartown Library.*

landscapes across New England, focusing on seaside scenes on Cape Ann and Martha's Vineyard.

Chris Baer, again: "Thompson declared he had become possessed by the spirit of a famous landscape painter." Frederic Louis Thompson was described as "supernaturally endowed with Gifford's artistic gifts." He devoted himself to landscape painting in Gifford's style. Additionally, Thompson said he could hear Gifford's voice. Thompson dreamed of paintings that Gifford had sketched out but not completed. It appears that Thompson hallucinated Gifford's work to some degree. "He sometimes felt as if he himself was Gifford."[69]

For more than a decade Thompson became a prolific success in the New York art world. The Thompsons summered on Cuttyhunk, another Elizabeth Island. In 1908, the couple befriended a wealthy patron, Horace Brookes, a quarter century older than the Thompsons. Now a threesome, over the years, they summered first in Menemsha, then on South Road, Chilmark, at Crow's Pocket Camp, their summer abode.

Time passed. Thompson no longer painted. By 1925, the couple had separated, then divorced. Thompson threatened his wife and sued Brookes, claiming the eighty-three-year-old had had an affair with his wife. Thompson was arrested for attempted murder and jailed in the Dukes County House of Correction before he was sent for evaluation to the Bridgewater Hospital for the Criminally Insane. Thompson was released to file more suits and countersuits. Brookes died in 1935 and Caroline nearly twenty years later.

The lawsuit between Frederic and Caroline Thompson is said to be the longest in Vineyard history. The saga of the psychic artist is both tormented and tantalizing, yet his artwork is captivating and still on the market.

THE KNIGHT OWEN MURDER is sad. It could be framed as a lovers' quarrel. Or it could be seen as a disoriented malcontent who maliciously took out his anger at an unwitting dupe. The story can be summarized as follows:

William Barry Owen was working for recording company, RCA, in London where he coined the phrase "his master's voice" in reference to his dog, Nipper. Owen made a fortune and became a prominent Vineyarder. (Owen Park, the land along the harbor, was donated to the town in his honor.)

Owen's son, Knight, was a ne'er-do-well. He drank too much and worked too little.

Knight Owen was a columnist for the *Vineyard Gazette*. He filed his last column, then went to visit a lady friend who lived with her children along Lake Tashmoo. Their relationship was one of companionship, not a vibrant love affair.

Living in a small cabin in the same area was Harold Look, a fisherman, a drinker and also a friend of Lydia Hyde, the woman both men admired. Look was not a stable worker; he helped Lydia Hyde inconsistently. Harold Look was jealous of Lydia's friendship with Knight Owen.

On the day in question, September 12, 1935, Owen had been drinking with nearby neighbors. He returned to his car, quite inebriated. Harold Look approached with his revolver drawn. Knight Owen had no idea his life was in danger. Look fired three shots; Owen slumped to the ground, dead.

Look knew he had committed murder. He turned himself in. When the police chief picked him up, Look requested they avoid driving by the house where his parents lived; he didn't want them to see him in custody. The police chief complied. Look was committed to Bridgewater State Hospital for the Criminally Insane; there he died three decades later, in 1964.

*This was only the fourth murder on Martha's Vineyard going back to the time of English settlement in 1642, and news of a shooting on the Vineyard drove the recent assassination of Huey Long, the governor of Louisiana, below the fold of major mainland newspapers. The papers decided that Knight Owen and Harold Look had competed for Lydia Hyde.*[70]

And that was the end of the life of Knight Owen.

THE MURDER OF CLARA Smith was especially grisly. Clara Smith of Dorchester visited the Vineyard for three weeks in the early summer of 1940. She was enrolled at the Rice School on East Chop in an elocution course designed to improve her diction as a Christian Science reader. Pearl Blakeney, a much younger friend from Canada, accompanied Mrs. Smith to the Vineyard.

On the morning of their last day, June 30, 1940, Clara Smith did not come down to breakfast. Blakeney thought "she stole a march on me," going off for an early morning walk. Instead, as Blakeney soon learned, Clara Smith had been brutally murdered the night before.

The women were lodged in separate rooms in the three-story dormitory on East Chop Drive, adjacent to the present East Chop Beach Club. (The foundation of the dormitory is still extant, adjacent to a wooden fence.) Other women in the dormitory heard sounds in the night, sounds of rumbling, moaning and calling out, attributed to nightmares.

Police were summoned. A murderer was arrested, jailed in Edgartown and tried in court. He was found innocent by a jury of his peers. Months later, no one had been arrested. Henry Beetle Hough, editor of the *Vineyard Gazette*, advocated that the district attorney pursue the case for an arrest. The murderer had disappeared.

Harold Tracy was a ne'er-do-well, itinerant electrician and small-time crook, from Vanceburg, Kentucky. When he felt the heat from a recent jewelry heist, he went to the local library, where he sought the most remote place to which he could escape. He arrived on the Vineyard in early June 1940 and was hired as an electrician by the Rice School.

Tracy was thirty-six. He picked up with a woman half his age, one Marjorie Massow. Mrs. Clara Smith, seventy-two and a widow, sought to discourage the romance. Tracy took offense.

Following an evening of heavy drinking, Tracy set off to visit his paramour at the Rice School dormitory. He ascended the stairs to the second floor. His girlfriend was on the third floor.

Tracy went into the room he supposed was that of his girlfriend. When he realized the woman in bed was Clara Smith, he became enraged. He strangled her. Then he disappeared.

While the district attorney made some futile attempts to solve the crime, Tracy left town. He was picked up for questioning four years later in Chicago. By then, the war was in full swing; both evidence and witnesses were hard to come by. Tracy was never charged.

Harold Tracy died in 1964 and was buried in Chicago.

~

WE WONDERED ABOUT THE Kennedy tragedy in 1969, driving off the bridge on Chappaquiddick. Holly Nadler, the renowned ghost lady, has a theory about that:

> *I addressed the possible element of the supernatural in the play of events* [on Chappaquiddick]. *The Oldsmobile went off the rails precisely where, many times beginning in the early 1900s, the inhabitants of Tom's Neck on Chappaquiddick, have glimpsed the ghost of one Charles Pease, murdered in the nearby woods.*[71]

What does the murder of Charles Pease in 1904 have to do with the death of Mary Jo Kopechne in 1969, you ask? Well, as Holly Nadler posits, perhaps the ghost of Charles Pease jumped in front of Kennedy's car and caused him to swerve off the Dike Bridge to avoid re-killing Mr. Pease. It's just a theory.

# 13

# PERSONAL TESTIMONIALS

A personal testimonial is where mystery confronts reality. Some people find solace in an unusual experience that happened to them. It may be a spiritual message, an unexpected coincidence or a haunted happening that cannot be resolved.

We present a number of situations to encourage the reader to relate to each one in as honest and realistic a manner as possible.

Here's a simple question submitted to the *Vineyard Gazette* regarding ghosts: "Talking with a friend was there a young ghost (possibly Edgartown) named Sally?" We tried to track down the person who submitted this inquiry without success.

Another comment was submitted regarding one of Holly Nadler's ghost stories, this from a woman in Washington, D.C.:

> *Dear Holly, I have another one for you....My grandparents, Marvin and Miriam Taylor bought "The Compass House" on North Water Street in Edgartown and retired there in the 1960's. The house came with a garden shed out back where we inquisitive grandchildren discovered a grim antique: The tombstone for infant Cyrus Pease Jernigan..."The blighted bud will bloom in heaven."*
>
> *We too shared quarters with a ghostly apparition. Every so often during the dead of night, her light footsteps would sound—pacing down the hallway between bedrooms, and back and forth again. She appeared to several of us, and to grandmother's holiday visitors. She was lovely,*

*young and pale, always in Victorian nightdress, and always the epitome of grief and mourning.*

We wonder if the previous young girl, Sally, is the same child walking around upstairs at the Compass House.

ONE SUMMER, MY WIFE, Joyce, cleaned a large house in Chilmark five days a week. Every Monday through Friday, she vacuumed, dusted, did laundry and scrubbed bathrooms and the large kitchen. By early August, she couldn't raise her right arm past shoulder height. She kept going to the chiropractor with the same complaint, but because she kept cleaning, there was no relief.

September arrived and the cleaning ended, but school started. When she went to write on the chalkboard, she had to hold her right arm up with her left hand. And of course, getting dressed was a problem.

One day, her friend Natalie asked if she wanted to go to the service the visiting healing priest was holding. Always curious, Joyce decided to join her. After prayers, hymns and testimonials, Father McDonough came down the aisle to bless everyone. When he came to their row, he blessed the first person and then Natalie. When he came to Joyce, he asked what was bothering her. She told him she couldn't raise her arm. He proceeded to pray over her, and she felt a warmth enveloping her and she sank into her seat. He told her to raise her arm. She could make a perfect high arc. Amen!

IN 2007, JOYCE LOST her father, a World War II vet, a caring father, a good husband. Three years later, within minutes of the same day, her mother, in failing health, also died.

We had been away for almost a week but managed to see her mother before she died. It was a Saturday, and Joyce told her she'd be back Monday. That Monday morning, her sister called to say their mother had died during the night. Joyce left to join her siblings to make funeral plans and returned Tuesday night to pack for the wake on Wednesday.

Because we get our mail at the post office, there was ten days' worth of mail on the dining room table near open windows. Adjacent to that table was another table that held various papers taken from the binder her parents had kept of World War II articles, photos and such. Joyce was in the bedroom, packing for her mother's impending funeral. I was sorting a week's worth of mail.

A paper from the pile of family items flitted into the air and fluttered to the floor. I picked it up and replaced it on the table, intent on getting things organized.

I continued to sort a week's worth of newspapers, bills, letters and advertisements. Again, that paper fell onto the floor. Annoyed, I picked it up to put it back on the table. I glanced at it. It was a telegram, dated January 2, 1944, from Joyce's father. It read, "Arrived safely."

Stunned, I brought it in to show my wife. Joyce's face filled with tears. "They're together! This is a message from my father that my mother arrived and they're together!"

Joyce is sure her father was yelling at Tommy, "For heaven's sake! Give it to Joyce!"

A few months later, Joyce had a dream that her father called and invited her to supper that night. His voice was crystal clear, as if he were right there.

ROGER BLAKE OF WEST Tisbury had always been a staunch Red Sox fan. He grew up in the post–World War II era dominated by Ted Williams, the last player to hit .400 (in 1941) and a hero to Sox fans during the darkest years before their World Series victory in 2004 after an eighty-six-year drought.

In the early 2000s, Roger knew Ted Williams was in failing health. Blake still maintained his love of his idol, nodding respects to the Splendid Splinter each morning as he plodded past a poster of Williams taped to his wall.

On the morning of July 5, 2002, Blake awoke to a muffled sound, a rustling he couldn't identify. Getting up, he meandered down the hall, and there on the floor was his Ted Williams poster.

Turning on the television, he learned Williams had passed away overnight. Was Ted sending a signal to his favorite fan?

When I shared this observation with Roger's son Eric, chief of the Oak Bluffs police, Eric believed it to be true. He said, "Look at the coincidence of John Adams and Thomas Jefferson, both dying on the same day, July 4, 1826, the fiftieth anniversary of the Declaration of Independence they wrote." From the Red Sox to the Declaration of Independence, coincidences occur.

ERIC CARLSON OF WEST Tisbury shared a couple of ghost stories. He recalled the saga of the Daggett House and the photo of the boy and the dog in the fire. He mentioned talking to the owner of the 1720 House in Vineyard Haven. He said there were ghosts associated with that establishment.

And Carlson said he had a friend in Aquinnah who claimed to have been pushed down a flight of stairs by an unseen ghostly influence. How many of these spectral stories are true ghost stories we leave to our readers.

TOM HALLAHAN OF OAK Bluffs spoke specifically about a time in his life, several years ago, when he felt a strong spiritual push. Tom was undergoing a rough time in his life. On a hopeful, but doubtful note, he was considering adopting a child.

Tom experienced an other-worldly experience, almost a direct statement—a voice, telling him to move ahead with the adoption. He took that message seriously and proceeded with the adoption of his son, Kiric.

Now, twenty years later, he is grateful for that spiritual messenger each time he thinks of Kiric, now a student in college. That spiritual message changed Tom's life. And Kiric's too!

WE SHARE A COUPLE of tales from an unnamed source who heard tales from a guard who worked with the inmates at the Dukes County House of Correction in the 1990s and 2000s.

> *Often the guards would see things pass on the security camera at night. They would make their rounds, but never found anything amiss. There were the usual lights flickering and a spot of light they could not explain. The story goes that an old guy hanged himself in the jail. And sometimes an inmate would complain about an eerie feeling he got from certain cells. Lots of odd things happened that could not be explained: a cool draft when the rest of the jail was hot. Why did that happen?*

Our reporter continued, "There's a brand-new yellow house on Waban Park in Oak Bluffs. Previously, there was an old rundown dilapidated house on the site. Lots of paranormal activity happened there. Lights would be on at night, but there was no electricity to the house, not even a light bulb." He added that creepy noises emanated from the building when you passed by; it was an eerie place, especially at night.

There was a ghost in the old Oak Bluffs School, on School Street. "No one ever saw him, but we knew he was there. Things went on there," said our informant. "When you go up the marble steps go left down the hall, then turn right, there was a classroom, and that's where things would happen."

On Chappy, people say the old William Martin house is haunted. Things go on there that you can't explain, like seeing someone sitting outside, and suddenly he wasn't there. It's like a ghost keeping an eye on his surroundings. Strange things happened that could not be explained.

In January 1981, Cynthia Farrington sat between two men in the front seat of a car. Suddenly, the car skidded on black ice. It proved to be a very serious auto accident. Cynthia was transported to Martha's Vineyard Hospital by ambulance, then airlifted to Falmouth Hospital, where she spent ten days in a coma. She was twenty-five. She remained unconscious, unresponsive and cold to the touch.

Cynthia recalled a vague sense from her coma that she experienced a very bright light. She saw her mother, rushed toward her and hugged her. "A feeling of protection and love washed over her."[72] Cynthia wanted to be with her mother.

Her mother hugged her. "'No," she said. "You need to go back. It's not your time!" her mother said kindly, wiping away Cynthia's tears. "You still have things to do."

In her description of her mother, Cynthia noted she was radiant and beautiful, and her red hair was impressive. (Cynthia's mother died of colon cancer in 1974, at the age of fifty.)

The bright white light began to fade, and Cynthia drifted into darkness. She spent an extended time in a coma. One recollection from the coma was hearing her boyfriend argue with someone over who was going in to see her in the ICU.

Eventually, Cynthia awoke. The hospital notes read that she "gradually woke up very lethargic and aphasic." Cynthia had a "Near death experience—NDE—and her experience of entering another realm were life-changing."[73]

Since this episode, some forty years ago, Cynthia has devoted her life to helping others. She is especially caring with people who are close to death, hospice patients, who are "on the threshold of death." Cynthia recognizes the increased importance of friends and family, of love and gratitude. She said, "There are no words in our earthly language to describe what I saw and felt. But…I do know that there is life after death."[74]

SUSAN DESMARAIS SHARED A couple of intriguing items of note. One time, she was recovering from surgery and feeling sorry for herself. Her cat jumped on her lap, cuddled her, comforting Susan in her hour of need. Their dog, who was dying, did not pay any attention.

Later, Susan spoke with a person who communicates with animals. The woman said the dog did not comfort Susan because he was allowing the cat to do what needed to be done. The dog wanted to be sure the cat would fill his role after he was gone. That comforted Susan even more.

Unfortunately, their faithful golden retriever had to be put down. It was a very sad experience. However, a few nights after the dog's death, Susan felt the dog nudge against her side while she was lying in bed. It was a comforting nudge, though it surprised her at first. It has continued to happen, and Susan speaks to Johnny's spirit.

Another incident was that Susan never had the chance to say goodbye to her father. He died rather suddenly. She has often dreamed of him. She's walking along a beach and sees her father ahead, on the shoreline. Before she can reach him, however, a fog bank moves in and obstructs her view.

One night, she was dreaming this dream. Her husband woke her up. She said, "Shh, I'm talking to my father." She went back to sleep and continued the dream, walking along the beach. This time, there was no fog bank, and Susan was able to meet her father, talk with him and say goodbye. She has never had the dream again.

Susan related an incident with her father's spirit:

> *One late summer evening, I was sitting on our screened porch in Oak Bluffs*
> *with a friend. I had just moved to the island and was getting to know my*

*new friend. We began talking about our families. We discovered we both had Irish daddies and were very close to them. For both of us, our dads died young. We raised a toast to our daddies saying that we each wished they could see us on the island. In that very moment, the recessed light directly above us began to flicker rapidly. There were three other lights on the same circuit which were not flickering and the bulbs were brand new. We grinned at each other and in unison said, "Hi Daddy." The light stopped flickering.*

~

On West Chop in 1995, Patty Egan was helping a friend open her family's summer house, a hundred-year-old mansion on the shore of West Chop.

"We spent the day cleaning the house," she recalled. "Then we went to bed. She was on the third floor; I was on the second floor. In the middle of the night, I heard furniture moving in the room above me."

The story continues: "In the morning I asked my friend, 'Why were you moving furniture in the middle of the night?' She asked me the same question. Neither of us had moved the furniture. It was a very strange situation."

Without equivocation, Patty said both she and her friend felt the house was haunted. Patty mentioned another house, on Tea Lane in Chilmark. "It is haunted," she said. "You know, I can feel it."

# 14

# CEMETERY TOURS

Cemetery tours bridge the past with the present, and on to the future. We don't know if there is life after death, but we want to cover all the bases by interring our loved ones in an appropriate setting. Walking through a cemetery links the people who went before us with who we are today. And if we take our role seriously and receptively, perhaps we'll have a glimpse of a ghost or an unknown energy that gives us pause. It may frighten us, or it may indeed give us a sense of hope in the faith of those who went before.

I was asked to offer a tour of Oak Grove Cemetery, across from the public library in Oak Bluffs. My walk among the graves has proved popular for young and old, tourist and local. We can do the tour in less than an hour and pause briefly at twenty or so graves, from the typical mariner of years gone by to the prominent author of twentieth-century fame. There's an opportunity to dig deeper on each grave we pass, but time and interest limit the length of each discussion.

Following is a brief summation of the loop we walk at Oak Grove thrice each summer.

The walk begins across from the Oak Bluffs Library. We stand by the monument to Shubael Norton, a nineteenth-century farmer who sold his land to the Oak Bluffs Land & Wharf Company. When the Company merged with the Wesleyan Camp Meeting Association, the town of Oak Bluffs was created.

Author Thomas Dresser gives tours of Oak Grove Cemetery in Oak Bluffs. While his focus is history, he's open to other sights and sounds. *Photo by Thomas Dresser.*

I speak about three eras of gravestone etchings, from the death's heads of the early eighteenth century to the winged cherubs later that century, culminating in the enlightened perspective of the urn and willow. We find stones of each era.

The graves of Benjamin Claghorn, his son and nephew are in the oldest section of the cemetery, dating from 1765. The three died in a marine mishap in Vineyard Sound.

From there, I meander by the grave of Della Hardman, a college art professor and later *Gazette* columnist, and Judge Leon Higgenbotham, who consulted with President Johnson following the assassination of Dr. Martin Luther King. And we sit on a stone bench by the grave of Tom Clancy, the author who loved his time on the Vineyard.

I mention Ralf and Luella Coleman of Boston Black Theatre fame; Albion Hart, who manned the information booth in downtown Oak Bluffs; Georgia Izett of Tivoli Inn; Dorothy West, the author; and the Denniston family, leaders in the African American religious heritage of twentieth-century Oak Bluffs. There are others, whalemen and auto mechanics, bankers and station managers, and we conclude at the grave of the world-renowned artist Lois Mailou Jones whose work encompassed Haiti, Africa and the States.

We don't encounter any ghosts along our route, but we've never entered the graveyard at night with kerosene lanterns and susceptible teenagers willing to squeal at anything out of the ordinary. Still, it's a popular tour, and we have branched out to Abel's Hill in Chilmark.

～

CHILMARK'S ABEL'S HILL CEMETERY is in the planning stage. Abel's Hill was named for Abel Wauwompuhque, a Wampanoag Native American who died in 1713. That makes Abel's Hill the oldest cemetery on Martha's Vineyard.

Like Oak Bluffs, this tour primarily speaks to the historically prominent people buried here: John Belushi, Lillian Hellman, Sarah and Lucy Adams, Rodney Dutcher, George Fred Tilton, Gale Huntington, Russell Hoxie and Everett Mayhew. One of the oldest graves is that of Experience Mayhew, the great-grandson of island progenitor Thomas Mayhew and author of *Indian Converts*.

Like Oak Bluffs, the tour can be completed in less than an hour and covers the highlights of several prominent people who deserve to be recognized. The tour is targeted to locals, but anyone, young or old, is welcome.

～

HOLLY NADLER IS KNOWN as the Ghost Lady of Martha's Vineyard. In one of her books, she is characterized as "one of the island's most knowledgeable residents when it comes to ghosts and gossip. In fact she is known locally as the Ghost Lady because of her two previous books, *Haunted Island* and *Ghosts of Boston Town*, and the haunted house walking tours she leads during the summer."[75]

Holly Nadler reached out to Karen Altieri and Gary Cook to assume operations of her ghost tours, which she had run for nearly twenty years. It was time to pass the Vineyard Ghost Walking Tours on to new faces. Holly gave her scripts to Gary and Karen, and they began their journey in 2010.

With a little advertising, they set up shop, leading tours in the three down-island towns: Oak Bluffs, Edgartown and Vineyard Haven. The first year was an unmitigated success; business was booming.

About twenty-five to thirty people gathered for each tour at 8:00 p.m., paid their fare and set off on a tour of the haunted sites in town. Karen and Gary carried kerosene lanterns and told their tales.

"That first year we both loved it," said Gary, wistfully. Many of their clientele came from inns, as the tour schedules were posted in local hotels. The draw was that the tour was family entertainment: kids are very open and receptive to ghost tours. Adults went along with the tales. And people who had been on other ghost tours shared their tales and experiences.

Oak Bluffs is the longest tour, ranging from the campground to the harbor and ending in Ocean Park at the Corbin-Norton House. One house in the campground has a rocking chair that rocks by itself. A streetlight in Oak Bluffs flickers on and off.

Vineyard Haven has a more compact route, including Main Street and up to the cemetery behind Town Hall, where intriguing sights are found. In the cemetery, one guy said, "I heard a bell behind me and felt someone put a hand on my shoulder."

Edgartown had two tours, one that includes sites on South Water Street. The group passes the "witch's house," where you hold your breath when you walk by. Faces have been seen in the windows.

The second Edgartown tour ranges along North Water Street, including the Daggett House. One unusual story was described by folks who stayed in a front room. Their son was playing in the living room; the parents heard him talking to someone. He told his parents that "a little boy was here." There was no little boy.

The tours are historical and educational entertainment. The guides explain about the oldest gravestones with etchings of skulls or death heads. Later stones bear suns and winged cherubs; more nineteenth-century stones include urns and willows.

Stories include people who were buried alive. Apparently, it was not uncommon. An undertaker would tie a string to the wrist of the deceased; if the person was not dead, they awoke and pulled a bell cord. We've heard the phrases: "saved by the bell" and "dead ringer." And the employee assigned to remain at the cemetery to listen for a ringing bell was assigned to the graveyard shift.

People take photos. They feel things. Orbs, colored circles and strange lights appear at nearly every location. "Every night someone captures an orb with a photo," said Gary. A red orb was seen at the top of the church steeple. Someone took a photo of a white conical figure outside the cemetery. At the Federated Church, Gary saw a photo by the altar, the image of a human, all in white. Gary has a photo of himself with an orange circle around his midsection.

A couple of stories guide Gary Cook shared occurred up-island. A woman was with friends at the Christiantown Cemetery in West Tisbury. She heard a whirring sound, and her arms were lifted out straight ahead of her; she could not move them. Her friends folded her into the car and took her to the hospital. After twenty minutes, she was back to normal.

A couple at Gay Head cliffs looked up in the sky. They heard a babble of indistinguishable voices, thousands of voices, but saw nothing. The voices came closer, passing overhead, then drifted off and beyond them and eventually vanished. The sky turned greenish. It was the sound of voices that they marveled at.

Vineyard Ghost Walking Tours run from mid-June to Labor Day, weather permitting. "If you love a good ghost story for fun, take one of the tours. In the dark, by light of a lantern, you'll learn some haunting tales that will send chills down your spine!"[76]

# 15

# GHOST STORIES

**M**artha's Vineyard has more than its share of ghost stories, tales of buried treasure, and supernatural lore in general," wrote the *Vineyard Gazette* more than eighty years ago. And ghost stories still attract the curious, intrigue the public and frighten the impressionable. We live on an island of vivid imagination, an island of hope and mystery, an island in the sea of humanity.

As noted earlier, a nonbeliever suggested an innkeeper told ghost stories to boost business. We don't refute that presumption, but we came across this comment from a currently operating hotel, in the heart of downtown Edgartown and, incidentally, founded by the progenitor of the Daggett House:

> *Formerly the Colonial Inn, our building has been at the center of Edgartown happenings since 1911. We can't say for sure whether we have ghosts, but one former manager did report a spooky hotel experience a few years back. If you're into ghost hunting, you wouldn't be the first to check in to our Edgartown hotel with Ouija board and EMF sensor in tow.*[77]

People are eager to hear ghost stories. And many Vineyarders are happy to share ghost stories. We dug up a couple of characters who enjoying sharing a story or two.

Manuel Swarz Roberts was the Vineyard's preeminent boatbuilder a century ago, working in the Old Sculpin Gallery on Edgartown Harbor. Manny shared many a ghost story with Milton Jeffers of Chappaquiddick, both how to find ghosts and how to send them on their way. Manny had seen spirits of Native Americans on Chappy. He kept those stories alive for Milton Jeffers, who shared those stories and more.

One story that was passed down from Chappaquiddick was that one day, Milton's father walked past three Native Americans, dressed in full regalia, leaning against a fence, passing a pipe. Jeffers passed them once, walked by again and even a third time. As Holly Nadler recounted Milton Jeffers's account on passing the Indians, "The three ancient tribesmen were still on the fence, passing the pipe. My father jogged home and went straight to bed."[78]

Then there was Benjamin Pease of Tom's Neck who related a Chappaquiddick tale or two. The old farmer said there are no hollows on Chappy, only "hollers," and one is the cry of an Indian squaw, murdered most horribly. The story goes that if you visit the site where she was killed on Christmas Eve, at midnight, you can hear her scream. Another tale is that as you approach a specific flat rock, slap it three times and ask, "What are you doing?" The answer will always come back, 'Nothing at all."

"Another Chappaquiddick story concerns a little, lame old man who appears at night near the estate of J. A. Jeremiah. Apparently this ghost of a patriarch, withered and bent, does nothing at all, but appears, walks a little distance, and vanishes."[79]

And then there's the late John Alley, who knew West Tisbury inside and out. He passed away in March 2020. In my last conversation with him, Alley acknowledged there are probably a number of ghost stories circulating in town, but the only one he felt comfortable sharing occurred right round the corner from Alley's Store, on Brandy Brow. As a boy, John never lingered on the path that meandered through Brandy Brow because the ghost of a woman who hanged herself would follow little children through the woods. John Alley claimed there's a plaque in her memory.

That brings to mind a poem of a West Tisbury house on Brandy Brow:[80]

*The Haunted House upon the hill*
*Has vanished from my sight,*
*It caught on fire when all was still*
*And burned up in the night;*
*The mossy roof has fallen in,*
*Its doors and windows gone,*
*It was a dismal looking place*
*For one to gaze upon.*

*And people told some awful tales,*
*That made one pulse's thrill,*
*About the sounds they heard at night*
*And spooks that walked the hill.*

Once he was older and presumably wiser, Alley realized his childhood fears were aroused by the wind rustling through the leaves on the trees. However, he was never 100 percent sure. It's worth wandering along Brandy Brow to experience whatever you can experience. You never know what you'll see, hear, smell or feel in the woods.

# EPILOGUE

*We have now arrived at the end of our journey, and must return whence we came, and if the traveler will take the author's advice he will return by the Middle Road, even if it is hilly and sandy, and discover a bit of the island for himself, for here is a terra incognita that the book has not touched on. It is likely that more buried treasure lies hereabout, why not discover it for yourself? And if no gold is found, the road furnishes a wealth of views that is worth a trip of many miles to enjoy.*[81]

Charles Hine urged his reader to savor the sandy, hilly Middle Road, arguably one of the more enjoyable island routes. These words mark the end of the road for Hine's tiny tome.

I consider the end of a book to be a graduation, a beginning to set off on more research, more reading, more review of the topic at hand. In this case, I suggest the reader explore more spectral sightings across the island. This book was compiled in the early months of 2020; undoubtedly, new experiences have occurred since then. Don't stop now. Pursue other books, other avenues of understanding.

The role of ghosts in our lives continues. Ghosts struggle to ferret out their incomplete lives. They are unaware they are alive or dead. Their existence must be a dream-like experience. Our job is to help them find their way.

You read this book because you are intrigued by poltergeists, paranormal experiences and out-of-this-world conceits. Keep your interest and curiosity in spirits alive. Don't be afraid to sit down at the bar of the Newes from

America. Order a mug of flip and have a word with a waitress about Helen. Wander the streets of Vineyard Haven past the Village Cemetery to feel the vibe of long-lost spirits. Visit the old Vanderhoop Homestead to sense the tragedy that still haunts the exquisite landscape. In each town and all over Martha's Vineyard are experiences to savor, explore and investigate. Don't stop now.

And wherever you go, whatever you do, have fun. Ghosts are not dangerous; they're struggling to complete their lives, to extricate themselves from whatever trauma killed them. Ghosts need our help, not our fears.

# NOTES

## Prologue

1. Haunted Martha's Vineyard Buildings & Martha's Vineyard Ghost Tour, www.vineyardsquarehotel.com.
2. Chris Hohmann, "Discover the Haunted History of Martha's Vineyard," A-A Island Blog, www.mvautorental.com.

## Chapter 1

3. Banks, *History of Martha's Vineyard*, 461.
4. Ibid., 464.
5. Nadler, *Haunted Island*, 146.

## Chapter 2

6. Hohmann, "Discover the Haunted History of Martha's Vineyard."
7. Ibid.
8. Holly Nadler, "Ghost Busing at the Kelley House," *MV Times*, January 14, 2014.
9. Stephanie Barnhart, "Real Haunted Stories—A Haunting in Martha's Vineyard," footballfoodandmotherhood.com.

## Chapter 3

10. "Ghost Stories," *Vineyard Gazette*, October 26, 1990.

## Chapter 4

11. "Names on the Land," *MV Quarterly*, November 2018.
12. "Commission Takes Steps to Protect Historic West Tisbury Roads," *Vineyard Gazette*, February 23, 2015.
13. Banks, *History of Martha's Vineyard*, 372.
14. "Between the Red Coats and the Deep Blue Sea," *MV Quarterly*, February 2018.
15. Banks, *History of Martha's Vineyard*, 374.
16. Hine, *Story of Martha's Vineyard*, 101.
17. "Hello from the Other Side," *MV Times*, October 24, 2017.
18. Hine, *Story of Martha's Vineyard*, 174.
19. Ibid., 125.

## Chapter 5

20. Hine, *Story of Martha's Vineyard*, 209.
21. Dresser, *Wampanoag Tribe of Martha's Vineyard*, 21.
22. Hine, *Story of Martha's Vineyard*, 17.
23. Ibid., 208–9.
24. Ibid., 193.
25. Ibid., 212.
26. Ibid., 204.
27. Ibid., 202.

## Chapter 6

28. Banks, *History of Martha's Vineyard*, 463.
29. Nadler, *Haunted Island*, 132–34.
30. Hine, *Story of Martha's Vineyard*, 190.
31. *Vineyard Gazette*, August 20, 1993.
32. *Vineyard Gazette*, April 8, 2010.

33. "Stories by Max Hart," *Vineyard Gazette*, October 27, 2005.
34. Nadler, *Haunted Island*, 99–100.
35. "Of Cottages and Camps: Memories of Renting," *Martha's Vineyard Magazine*, March 1, 2016.

## Chapter 7

36. Ibid.
37. Hine, *Story of Martha's Vineyard*, 106.
38. Hohmann, "Discover the Haunted History of Martha's Vineyard."
39. Nadler, *Vineyard Confidential*, 115.
40. "Talking About a Revolution," *Martha's Vineyard Magazine*, September–October 2007.

## Chapter 8

41. "This Was Then: Island School History," *Martha's Vineyard Times*, September 11, 2019.
42. Norton, *Walking in Vineyard Haven*, 173.

## Chapter 9

43. "Hollers," *Vineyard Gazette*, April 30, 1937.
44. *Vineyard Gazette*, October 25, 1985; republished October 24, 2019.
45. "Hollers," *Vineyard Gazette*, April 30, 1937.
46. "Out Alone: The Ghost Hunter's Tale," *Vineyard Gazette*, October 25, 2007.

## Chapter 10

47. Hine, *Story of Martha's Vineyard*, 66.
48. Ibid., 68.
49. Banks, *History of Martha's Vineyard*, 462.

## Chapter 11

50. Hine, *Story of Martha's Vineyard*, 25–27.
51. Ibid.
52. Ibid., 143.
53. Ibid., 198.
54. "This Was Then: Money Digging," *Martha's Vineyard Times*, May 8, 2019.
55. Hine, *Story of Martha's Vineyard*, 48.
56. Ibid., 49.
57. "Oak Bluffs Town Column," *Vineyard Gazette*, November 29, 2018.
58. Dresser, *Martha's Vineyard in World War II*, 164–65.
59. "Jimmy Morgan," *MV Magazine*, July 1, 2008.
60. Dresser, *Travel History*, 122.
61. Dresser, *Wampanoag Tribe*, 36.
62. Nadler, *Vineyard Confidential*, 83.
63. "The First English Settlers of Martha's Vineyard," *MV Quarterly*, November 2018.
64. Ibid.

## Chapter 12

65. Dresser, *Whaling on Martha's Vineyard*, 121.
66. Ibid., 123.
67. "Island Crucible," *MV Magazine*, January 12, 2016.
68. Baer, *Martha's Vineyard Tales*, 182.
69. Ibid., 182–83.
70. "Night Falls," *MV Magazine*, September 1, 2006.
71. Nadler, *Vineyard Confidential*, 117.

## Chapter 13

72. Rushnell, *How Godwink Moments Guide Your Journey*, 194.
73. Ibid., 196.
74. Ibid.

## Chapter 14

75. Nadler, *Vineyard Confidential*, author's notes.
76. Hohmann, "Discover the Haunted History of Martha's Vineyard."

## Chapter 15

77. Haunted Martha's Vineyard Buildings & Martha's Vineyard Ghost Tour.
78. Nadler, *Haunted Island*, 158.
79. "Hollers," *Vineyard Gazette*, April 30, 1937.
80. ENH, undated issue of *Vineyard Gazette*.

## Epilogue

81. Hine, *Story of Martha's Vineyard*, 219–20.

# BIBLIOGRAPHY

*Books*

Baer, Chris. *Martha's Vineyard Tales*. Guilford, CT: Globe Pequot, 2018.

Banks, Charles. *The History of Martha's Vineyard*. Boston: George H. Dean, 1911.

Dresser, Thomas. *Disaster Off Martha's Vineyard*. Charleston, SC: The History Press, 2012.

———. *Hidden History of Martha's Vineyard*. Charleston, SC: The History Press, 2017.

———. *Martha's Vineyard in World War II*. Charleston, SC: The History Press, 2014.

———. *A Travel History of Martha's Vineyard*. Charleston, SC: The History Press, 2019.

———. *The Wampanoag Tribe of Martha's Vineyard*. Charleston, SC: The History Press, 2011.

———. *Whaling on Martha's Vineyard*. Charleston, SC: The History Press, 2018.

Hine, Charles. *The Story of Martha's Vineyard*. New York: Hine Brothers, 1908.

Jasper, Mark. *Haunted Cape Cod and the Islands*. Eastham, MA: On Cape Publications, 2002.

Nadler, Holly. *Haunted Island*. Camden, ME: Down East Books, 2014.

———. *Vineyard Confidential*. East Peoria, IL: Down East Books, Versa Press, 2006.

Norton, James. *Walking in Vineyard Haven, Massachusetts*. Edgartown, MA: Martha's Vineyard Historical Society, 2000.

Rushnell, Squire. *How Godwink Moments Guide Your Journey*. New York, NY: Howard Books, 2012.

## Periodicals

*Martha's Vineyard Magazine*
*Martha's Vineyard Times*
*MV Quarterly*
*Vineyard Gazette*

# INDEX

# ABOUT THE AUTHOR

**A**ll his life, Thomas Dresser understood the hard facts and definitive words of history; he never saw a ghost and didn't believe until he sat down to write this book. Interviews and research indicate something is out there. Now he is a believer.

TOM GREW UP IN central Massachusetts and moved to Martha's Vineyard in the '90s to be with his childhood friend Joyce. Married over twenty years, they are very involved with five children and nine grandchildren. Their lives are full.

Living on Martha's Vineyard has given Tom a better grasp of the value a tranquil environment has on peace of mind. Living in a harmonious relationship has given Tom the opportunity to blossom in retirement. Together, Tom and Joyce have carved out a lifestyle neither suspected when they first met in Holden Junior High in the late 1950s. Sometimes life hands you a bag of coal; sometimes it's a bag of hope.

Author Thomas Dresser honors his parents who died in their sixties. Their spirits survive in his writing. *Photo by Joyce Dresser.*

*Also by Thomas Dresser*

*African Americans of Martha's Vineyard*
*Disaster off Martha's Vineyard*
*Hidden History of Martha's Vineyard*
*Martha's Vineyard: A History*
*Martha's Vineyard in World War II*
*Music on Martha's Vineyard*
*Mystery on the Vineyard*
*The Rise of Tourism on Martha's Vineyard*
*A Travel History of Martha's Vineyard*
*The Wampanoag Tribe of Martha's Vineyard*
*Whaling on Martha's Vineyard*
*Women of Martha's Vineyard*

For more, visit thomasdresser.com